THE CHARACTER OF JESUS

CHARLES EDWARD JEFFERSON
PASTOR OF BROADWAY TABERNACLE
NEW YORK CITY

TABLE OF CONTENTS

PREFACE

The following discourses were delivered in the Broadway Tabernacle on the Sunday evenings between January first and Easter of the winters of 1907 and 1908, twelve of them in the former year and fourteen of them in the latter. They are simple studies in the character of Jesus, the twofold purpose of the preacher being to incite professing Christians to a deeper devotion to their Master, and to awaken in non-Christians a desire to know more of the founder of the Christian church, and to persuade them to become his followers. The congregations were composed largely of young men, not a few of them being students. It is in response to numerous requests of these young men that the sermons are now published. No preacher speaks entirely as he writes, or writes altogether as he speaks. The sermons have been allowed to retain for the most part the unstudied form of extemporaneous discourse, not even the repetitions being eliminated, which are inevitable in a course of sermons addressed to a congregation changing from week to week. Questions of authorship and text were all left untouched, as having but slight interest for a majority of those who heard the sermons. After a study of a considerable portion of the voluminous New Testament criticism of the last thirty years, the preacher has no hesitation in asserting his conviction that the Gospels give us credible history, and that they, while not inerrant, present us a portrait of Jesus sufficiently accurate to do the work which God intends it shall do. In spite of all that has been written to the contrary, the preacher has found no solid reason for thinking that the reliable passages in the Gospels are few, or that the portrait is a work of imagination inspired and colored by affection. The men who wrote the Gospels are in his judgment more trustworthy than any of the men who have endeavored to discredit them. The two opening sermons were preached, one at the beginning of 1907, the other at the beginning of 1908.

I: INTRODUCTORY

"Behold the Man!"
— John xix: 5.

Let us think together on these Sunday evenings of the Character of Jesus. You will observe the limitation of the subject. Jesus alone is too great a theme to be dealt with in a course of lectures. There are, for instance, the Ideas of Jesus, the principles which he enunciated in his sermons and illustrated in his parables. This is a great field, and fascinating, but into it we cannot at present go. The Doctrines of Jesus, the things he taught of God and the soul, of life and death, of duty and destiny: this also is another field spacious and rewarding, but into it we cannot enter. We might think of the Person of Jesus, meditate upon his relations to the Father, and to the Holy Spirit, and to us, and ponder the immeasurable mystery of his personality — this is what thoughtful minds have ever loved to do. But upon this vast field of thought we also turn our backs in order that we may give ourselves undividedly to the Character of Jesus. By "character" I mean the sum of the qualities by which Jesus is distinguished from other men. His character is the sum total of his characteristics, his moral traits, the features of his mind and heart and soul. We are to think about his quality, his temper, his disposition, the stamp of his genius, the notes of his spirit, and the form of his conduct. In one sense our studies will be elementary. We are to deal with the ABC's of Christian learning. This is the logical beginning of all earnest study into the meaning of the Christian religion. Before we are rightly prepared to listen to the ideas of Jesus we must know something of what Jesus is. The significance of what a man says depends largely upon what he is. Two men may say precisely the same thing; but if one is known to be a fool, his words make no impression on us; if the other is known to be wise and good we give him close and sympathetic attention. A man is better able to appreciate the ideas of Jesus if he first of all becomes acquainted with Jesus' character.

To begin with the character of Jesus is to adopt the scientific method of study. The scientist of to-day insists upon studying phenomena. What he wants is data, and from these he will draw his conclusions. No scientist can begin his work unless put in possession of definite and concrete facts. There is a general opinion abroad that Christianity is something very much in the air. It is vague and nebulous, cloudy and indeterminate, something beautiful as the mist with the morning sun playing on it, but also like the mist very thin and high above the world in which men live. But in this course of lectures I do not ask you to think about visions or conceptions, principles or relations; I call your attention to a few definite and clean-cut facts. This man Jesus was an historic character. He lived his life upon this earth. In his passage from the cradle to the grave he manifested certain traits and dispositions which it is our purpose to study. If we were to attempt to deal with all his sayings, we should find many of them hard to understand, and if we should attempt to grapple with his personality, we should find ourselves face to face with mysteries too deep to be fathomed; but in dealing with his character we are handling something concrete and comprehensible. Let us place ourselves before him and permit him to make upon us whatsoever impression he will.

Not only is this the scientific method, it is also the New Testament method. It was just in this manner that the disciples came to know Jesus. They did not begin with the mystery of his person, nor did they begin with sayings which were hard for them to understand. They began simply by coming near him, looking at him with their eyes, listening to him with their ears. It is with a shout of exultation that the beloved apostle in the first of his letters says, "We handled him with our hands." It would seem from the New Testament that Jesus desires men to come to the truth which he is to give to the world by a knowledge of his character. When two young men one day followed him along the bank of the Jordan, and he turned upon them and said: "Whom are you looking for?" and they replied, "Where do you live?" his answer was, "Come and see." They remained with him for the rest of the day, and the result of their first meeting was that they wanted their comrades to come and see him also. And from that day to this the cause of Christianity has advanced in the world simply because those who have already seen him have wanted others to come and share their experience.

If this was the method of approach to Christianity in the first century, why is it not the best approach for our time? Christianity in the course of its development has taken on many forms and has gathered up into itself many things which are non-essential. The result is that thousands are bewildered, not knowing what to think or what to do. Many have been offended by Christianity because they have attempted to enter it through the ecclesiastical door. They have come to the religion of Jesus through some professing Christian who has been inconsistent or hypocritical, and simply one such disastrous experience is sufficient sometimes to keep a man away from Christ through his entire life. Sometimes it is no individual Christian, but the local church as a body that gives the offence. It may be that the church is dead or that its leading men are corrupt or that its preacher is ignorant and does not have the Christian spirit or the Christian outlook; in which case the total impression made by the church is disastrous, and the soul is repelled. There are many men who are not Christians to-day because it was their peculiar misfortune to come at a critical period in their life in contact with a church which was lacking in Christian sympathy and devotion. There are others who have attempted to get into Christianity through the dogmatic door. They have come to the dogmatic statements of the Christian church, the doctrines formulated by church councils and theologians, and by these they have been offended. Their reason has been repelled and their heart has been chilled. Let me suggest that there is another door: the character of Jesus. Neither professing Christians nor dogmatic statements are the door of the Christian religion. The founder of Christianity says: "I am the Door." It may be that some man in the congregation who has been made cynical by professing Christians, or sceptical by church dogmas may find that he is neither sceptical nor cynical after he has studied the character of Jesus. For after all, to be a Christian is not to be like other professing Christians, or to accept ecclesiastical propositions; to be a Christian is to admire Jesus so sincerely and so fervently that the whole life goes out to him in an aspiration to be like him.

This is a very opportune time in which to study the character of Jesus because it is in our day and generation that he has appeared with new glory before the eyes of the world. We who are now living can know him, if we will, better than he has ever been known since the days of the apostles. There have been three stupendous pieces of work accomplished within the last seventy years. Two of them are well known to everybody, the third is recognized by comparatively few. The first magnificent accomplishment of the last seventy years is the construction of the palace of science. This great enterprise has been carried forward by a host of men of genius who have thrown into their work the heroism of prophets and the enthusiasm of apostles. Almost the entire structure of the palace of science has been built up within the last seventy years. How glorious, how dazzling it is, I need not attempt to describe, for it has caught and holds the eyes of the world. The second great achievement of the last seventy years is the development of material civilization. Within these years have come the steamship, the railroad, the telegraph, the telephone, and a thousand other inventions by means of which the face of the world has been transformed and the habits of men have been revolutionized. This is a miracle which is also known to all. But there is a third piece of work even more wonderful and more far-reaching in its effects than these other two, and that is the work which has been done by a great army of scholars on both sides the sea in bringing Jesus of Nazareth out of the shadows and out of the clouds in which he had been hidden, and placing him once more before the world.

It was in 1835 that Strauss published his first edition of the "Life of Jesus," and from that day to this the world has been studying the character of the Man of Galilee with an interest which has been constantly deepening, and with a zeal that shows no abatement. The Gospels have been subjected to a scrutiny which has been given to no other writings. The libraries and the mounds and the tombs have been ransacked for manuscripts. The manuscripts have been brought together and carefully compared and each minutest variation has been noted and pondered. Every paragraph has been sifted and every sentence has been weighed, every word has been analyzed and every syllable has been examined and cross questioned. The amount of labor bestowed upon the New Testament within the last seventy years is amazing and incalculable. Men have not been contented with studying the manuscripts, they have studied the land in which Jesus lived; they have measured it from north to south and from east to west with a surveyor's chain. They have taken the heights of the hills and the mountains, and the depths of the rivers and seas. With pick and shovel, they have gone down into the earth in search of material to throw additional rays of light upon this man who has made the land "Holy." The first century of our era has been studied as no other century since time began. The customs of the people, their clothing, their houses, every feature of their social and political and ecclesiastical life, everything that they read and everything that they said, and everything that they did has been analyzed, discussed, explained, illustrated, photographed, and scattered broadcast in the hope that this might bring men closer to Jesus. The civilization of the first century in Palestine has been subjected to a scrutiny and analysis which no other civilization has ever known. The printing-presses on both sides the sea are flooding the world with books about the life and the times of Jesus. And the result is he looms colossal before the eyes of the world. It is not simply the church that sees him; all men can see him now. He has broken out of ecclesiastical circles; he walks through all cities and lands. All sorts and conditions of men have come to admire him. Those who despise the church respect him, those who deny Christian dogmas bow before him. The great unchurched classes who care nothing for anthems or sermons break into applause at the mention of his name. Many of them see him dimly, many of them have caught only a glimpse of his face and his heart, but everybody knows that he is the man who went about doing good. Everywhere his name is reverenced. It is fitting that in these opening years of the new century we should endeavor to gain a clearer apprehension of the range of his mind and the reach of his heart. How are we to get our information? There are six channels through which light will come. We may come to know him through the words he spoke, through the deeds he did, and also through his silences. We may know him also by the impression which he made first upon his friends and secondly upon his foes, and thirdly upon the general body of his contemporaries.

It awes me when I think of the great company that no man can number to which I ask you to join yourselves in this study of the character of Jesus. Let your mind roam over the last nineteen hundred years, and think of the artists who have stood before him, seeing in him new revelations of beauty; think of the poets who have stood before him and have caught inspiration for their songs; think of the musicians who have stood before him and who have worked the impression which he made upon them into tones which lift the heart and set it dreaming; think of the philosophers who have stood before him and meditated on the great ideas which found expression on his lips; think of the unlettered men and women, the great crowd of peasants, plain working people, descendants of the shepherds that heard the angels singing, who have bowed in adoration before him and found rest from their weariness and strength in their weakness. And then let your mind run out into the centuries that are coming and think of the countless generations of men and women who are still to stand before this matchless figure, drinking in inspiration with which to live their life and do their work. If you can see in your imagination this great procession which has been and the greater procession which is yet to be, you will take your places with reverent spirit as once again we attempt to study the character of the man who compels the heart to cry out, "Master!"

II: REASONS FOR OUR STUDY

"Come and see."
— John i: 46.

I INVITE you to contemplate with me the character of Jesus. Many of you have studied him under the leadership of others, come with me for a little interval and let us study him again. The time is ripe for a restudy of his character and career. We have fallen upon distracted and distracting days. The world is crying out for something, it scarce knows what. Wealth has come, but the heart is hungry; knowledge has come, but life for many has slipped into a riddle and delusion. The world is filled with the inventions of human skill and genius, but there is a vast emptiness which neither science nor art is able to fill.

One of the notes of twentieth century life is discontent. Some of us are discontented with ourselves. We are restless, unsatisfied, bewildered. We carry with us a consciousness of failure. We feel we are falling short of what we ought to be. Life in spite of our efforts is meagre and disappointing. Loaded with many possessions we cry, "What lack I yet?" It may be wise, therefore, to turn aside from the path we have been travelling and listen for a season to Jesus of Nazareth. It may be that he has the secret for which we have been searching. On opening the New Testament the first face which fronts us is his and the first words which greet us come from his lips. He says, "Come unto me and I will give you rest, I am the bread of life, I am the Light of the world, If any man thirst let him come unto me and drink. My peace I give unto you. You shall receive power. You shall rejoice." Bread and water, light and rest and peace and power and joy, are these not the seven elemental blessings which make human life complete? If this man promises to give us the things which the soul most desires, it is worth while to study his method and find out, if we can, how his proffered gifts can be most speedily obtained. On approaching him we hear him saying: "Follow me! Learn of me! Eat me! Abide in me!" It would seem that he offers us all good things on condition that we become like him. But what is he like? What is his disposition, temper, attitude, nature? Surely all who are discontented with themselves will want to study the character of Jesus.

There are others of us who are discontented, not so much with ourselves as with the world. The time is out of joint, and we are sick at heart because no one seems to be wise or strong enough to set it right. Government is corrupt, the church seems dead or dying, the home is a failure or scandal, society is superficial and tainted, the social order is ready for the burning, the economic system is a burden and curse, the whole framework of the world needs to be reconstructed, and, alas, who is sufficient for so herculean a task? The men with panaceas are loud-mouthed and confident, the prophets of reform are vociferous and ubiquitous, but unfortunately they do not agree among themselves, and the remedies when applied are impotent to cure. The medicines do not seem to be powerful enough, and the doctors stand by the bedside of feverish and delirious humanity, outwitted, discredited, dumfounded. Modern civilization has become a tower of Babel, and the air is so filled with theories of social amelioration and programmes of industrial reorganization that the clearest headed are bewildered by the din and tumult, not knowing in which direction deliverance must be sought.

When we open our New Testament, we find a man looking at us who although not a professional revolutionist has been the cause of many revolutions, and who although not a disturber of the peace has repeatedly turned the world upside down. He is not numbered among the radicals because in his radicalism he outstrips them all. He dares to reverse all human standards, confounds the wise by things which are foolish and confounds things which are mighty by the things which are weak. He has much to say about authority and power, and it is his claim that he can make all things new. The writers of history have confessed that he overturned the Roman Empire and has given to Europe and America a civilization unlike any which the world has ever known. If his ideas have in them the force of dynamite, and if his personality has power to change the policy of empires and even the temper of the human heart, it may be that this man is the very man the modern world is looking for in its wild quest for a way of deliverance from its miseries and woes. Surely all of those who are sick of the world as it is and who long for the coming of a world which shall be better, must, if they are wise, come to Jesus of Nazareth for his secret of pulling down the strongholds of iniquity and establishing righteousness and peace in the earth.

When we study his method, we discover that his supreme concern is for the rightness of heart of the individual man. This moulder of empires gives himself to the task of moulding individual men. This arch revolutionist starts his conflagrations in the individual soul. He draws one man to him, infuses into him a new spirit, sends him after one brother man, who in time goes after a third man, and this third man after a fourth, and thus does he weld a chain by means of which Caesar shall be dragged from his throne. Strange as it may seem, he has nothing to say about heredity, and stranger still nothing to say about environment. He keeps his eyes upon the soul, and by changing this he alters the environment and also the currents of the blood down through many generations . When we speak of environment, we think of the physical surroundings: the paving in the street, the sewerage, the architecture of the houses, and the lighting of the rooms. We are convinced that with better sewerage and better ventilation and better lighting the plague of humanity would be speedily abated. But this Reformer of Nazareth acts and speaks as though environment is not a matter of brick and plaster but rather of human minds and hearts. Men are made what they are, not by pavements and houses, but by the men among whom they live. Would you change the environment, then begin by a transformation of men; and would you transform men, then begin by a transformation of some particular man. It is by the changing of the character of a man that we change the character of other men, and by changing the character of many men we change the character of institutions and ultimately of empires and civilizations. When Jesus says, "Behold I make all things new," he lays his hand on the heart of a man. It is out of the heart the demons proceed which tear humanity to pieces, and it is out of the heart that the angels come which restore the beauty and peace of Paradise.

Here then is Jesus' own secret for making an old world over. He will introduce golden ages by giving individuals a character like his own. His character is a form of power mightier than the legions of Caesar or the wisdom of the greatest of the schools. We who are most discontented with the world and most eager to banish its tyrannies and abuses may profitably give our days and our nights to the study of the character of Jesus, for through this the burdened world is to pass forward into a brighter day. There are many fussy and noisy workers, many a blatant and spectacular leader, reformers are often plausible and dashing, and revolutionists impress us by their schemes of creating a world which is new, but after all there is no more effective worker for the world's redemption than the man or woman who in high or obscure places, strives, in season and out of season, to persuade men to conform their lives to the pattern presented to us in the character of Jesus; and no one is advancing so swiftly toward the golden age as the man or woman who by prayer and daily effort endeavors to build up in mind and spirit the virtues and graces of the Man of Galilee.

Here then we find the supreme mission of the Christian clergyman: it is to help men to fall in love with the character of Jesus. The Bible is an invaluable book chiefly because it contains a portrait of Jesus. The New Testament is immeasurably superior to the Old because in the New Testament we have the face of Jesus. The holy of holies of the New Testament is the Gospels because it is here we look directly into the eyes of Jesus. We often speak of the Gospel: What is it? Jesus!

Let us come now a little closer and ask, What is it in Jesus which is most worth our study? A deal of attention is being given to the circumstances which formed the framework of his earthly life. Many men are working on the chronology and others are at work on the geography, and others are interested in the robe and the turban and the sandals. Photographers have photographed every landscape on which he ever looked, and every scene connected with his work or career. Painters have transferred the Palestinian fields and lakes and skies to canvas, and stereopticon lecturers have made the Holy Land the most familiar spot on earth. Writers of many grades have flooded the world with descriptions of customs and houses, of fashions and ceremonies, and amid such a mass of drapery and upholstery we are in danger of losing the man Jesus. We may become so interested in the fringes and tassels of his outer life as to miss the secret which his heart has to tell. Many an hour has been spent upon the outer trappings of Jesus' life which might better have been employed in the earnest study of his mind and heart. Palestine has no interest for us except in so far as it assists us to understand what Jesus was and did. The temporal and local and provincial may be interesting, but it is not important. It is the character of Jesus which has unique and endless significance, and to this then every earnest mind and heart should turn. The pictures have no value unless they carry us deeper into the soul of the man. It is surprising what meagre materials we have to deal with in the study of Jesus. The New Testament writers were not interested in trifles. They cared nothing for his stature, the clothes he wore or the houses he lived in. He had none of the things which biographers are wont to expatiate upon to the extent of many chapters. He had no lineage to boast of. His friends were all obscure. He held no office either in church or state. He had no prestige of wealth and no repute for learning. He was born in a stable, worked in a carpenter's shop, taught for three years, and then died on a cross. The external is reduced to its lowest, circumstances are commonplace and meagre, the framework of life is narrow and ungilded. The New Testament was written by men who were determined that we should fix our eyes on the man. They wish us to catch the beat of his heart, the swing of his mind, the orbit of his ideas. Everything is minimized and subordinated to that which is central and all important, the texture of his spirit and the attitude of his personality. With one accord they cry, "Behold the man!" They want us to know how he looked at things, how he felt toward things, and how things affected him. In a word, they want us to know his character. Let us accept their invitation and come and see.

Some of us have studied this man Jesus for many years. It is we who have the keenest desire to study him again. We shall find in him now things which we have never seen before. The eyes are always changing and the heart expands with the increase of the years. We climb to higher levels of knowledge through study and experience. The time will never come when we shall not relish the study of this man. He is the way to God. It is impossible to become too familiar with the way. He is the express image of the Father's person. The more we study him the richer is our knowledge of the heart of God. He has declared the Father. The more fully we understand him the deeper we see into the heart of Deity. If he and the Father are one, then to know him is indeed life eternal. If he is the author and finisher of faith, we need to see his unclouded face if we are to run with patience the race that is set before us. If we are to be changed from character to character by looking at his character, then every hour we spend in making that character clear and beautiful to our heart is blessed. The beloved disciple used to say, "We beheld his glory." They gazed upon him as he worked and talked and sang and prayed, and the very memory of what they saw lifted life to new altitudes and dimensions. The ripest and most experienced Christians are readiest to accept the invitation, "Come and see."

Some of us have studied this portrait only a little. Jesus is a name, but as a person he is shadowy and unreal. His face has become obscured. Our heart does not feel his power. We are not indifferent to him, but we have no keen sense of loyalty to him, no purifying consciousness of adoration. We need to study him afresh. It may be that as we study him he will step out of the picture and take his place by our side. Not until we know him as a comrade do we get from him what he has to give. Because his face is dim we are often depressed and defeated. We are always faint in life's hard places unless we are close enough to catch the light of his eye and feel the strong beating of his unconquerable heart. It may be that to some of us he has been petrified into a dogma. It is a great day for the soul when Jesus stands before it for the first time as a man. Never shall I forget when for the first time he became human to me. It was on a Saturday evening when a great teacher was expounding the words, "Father, save me from this hour." In a flash I saw Jesus shrinking, and the fountains of my heart were opened.

Some of us have scarcely studied him at all. All we know we know by hearsay. We are prejudiced against this Jesus of Nazareth. His face has been distorted partly by the misrepresentations of others and partly by our own idiosyncrasies. It may be that during this study some of us shall see him for the first time as he is.

There are those who do not like metaphysics; let them come and look upon a full-statured man. They do not care for doctrine, let them study a life. They are not interested in dogma, let them fix their gaze upon a person. If the word "revelation" has had to them a mysterious or theological sound, let them contemplate the crowning revelation — the revelation made in the character of a man.

We shall not discuss the question how the Gospel portrait got here. It is enough for our present purpose to know that it is here. It has been in the world for nearly nineteen hundred years and through all that period nothing has been added to it and nothing has been taken away. If any one should care to point out minor defects in the workmanship, it is enough to say that the portrait does its work. It nourishes faith in God. It keeps the fires of hope and gladness burning on the altar. Men have various theories of the portrait and make divers criticisms of it, but the world is dominated by it. I ask you to look at it. Other men are looking at it. They are looking at it all round the globe. Millions feel while looking at it that in this portrait they get the largest disclosures of the mind and purpose of the Eternal. It is indisputable that this portrait draws many hearts nearer to God. It may draw you. Only look at it. Other things are passing, but this portrait is a reality which abides. Many a treasure has been melted in the crucible, but not this. In many circles the Bible has been growing less and the church also has been dwindling, but everywhere the wide world over the character of Jesus has been looming larger before the eyes of thinking men. By looking at it, it may grow also upon you.

And may I ask you also to pray while you look. The depth to which you see into a mind or heart depends upon what you bring with you to the contemplation of it. You cannot appreciate the masterpiece of a musician unless you have music in you, or the painting of an artist unless you have in you something of the temperament which the artist has, nor can you understand a character unless you are akin to it in the deepest tendencies and aspirations of your being. The masters of music and art and life reveal themselves only to those who in some measure share their spirit. Would you study the character of Jesus with largest profit, you must respond to that which was dominant in his life. He was preeminently a man of prayer. His was the reverent heart and his look was ever upward. They who pray breathe the atmosphere in which he lived and take the attitude by which they are best fitted to understand his deeds and sayings. In studying a person spiritual harmony is everything. James lived under the same roof with Jesus but did not understand him. Paul lived far from him but understood him completely. Understanding souls is not a matter of physical proximity or intellectual effort: everything depends on insight and spiritual sympathy. In studying Jesus men ought always to pray and not to faint.

III: SOURCES

"These are written that ye may believe that Jesus is the Christ, the Son of God." — John xx: 31.

Where can we find a subject more interesting than the Character of Jesus? It is fascinating to every human being who has the slightest ambition to advance in culture, or who has the smallest capacity for apprehending things which are of deep and enduring significance. Simply as a piece of biography what a wonderful story this is, how exciting his life, how tragic his death! Whether a man is a Christian or not he must, unless thoroughly hardened by prejudice, take an interest in the life of Jesus. No man or woman of intellect can remain unmoved by the death of Socrates. The prison in which he died is one of the holy places of history. So long as men have minds to think and hearts to pity, they will stand in awe before the old Greek philosopher while he drains the fatal cup. But the death of Jesus is more tragic than the death of Socrates. Who is not interested in the death of Julius Caesar? When will Mark Antony's speech cease to stir the blood? So long as men are human they will stand awestruck in the presence of that great tragedy enacted in the Roman capitol. But the death of Jesus is more tragic than the death of Caesar. Moreover, Jesus of Nazareth is the starting point of a thousand influences. The whole world of the last nineteen hundred years becomes unintelligible unless one knows something about him. How can you understand the great art galleries of the world, filled as they are with pictures of his face, and pictures of his mother, and pictures of his disciples, unless you know who he was and what he said and what he accomplished? Step out of the art galleries into the libraries and how will you understand the great books of history unless you are familiar with his career, for every book is full of his name. Step out of the world of books into the world of men and things, walk along the streets, how will you account for St. Patrick's Cathedral and the Cathedral of St. John the Divine; and all the hundreds of churches and missions scattered over this land unless you know something of the man from whose heart they proceeded and by whose name they are known. We have a theme that must be of interest to every human being.

But as soon as we come to the careful study of the life of Jesus, we are subjected to a series of surprises. The first surprise is that the biography of this man is confined within such narrow limits. If you wish to study the life of Abraham Lincoln, you must consult many volumes. The life of George Washington cannot easily be put into one book. Hundreds of volumes have been written about Napoleon and Frederick the Great and Caesar. But the biography of Jesus is confined to one little book that can be bought for six cents and carried in the pocket. This is the surprising thing that all the story of his life is contained in this one book. There were many Greek writers living in the days of Jesus, but not one of them wrote his life, so far as any scholar knows. Not a scrap of Jesus' biography at the hands of a Greek poet or historian has come down to us. There were many Roman writers living when Jesus preached in Palestine, they were writing on many different personages and on manifold subjects, but not one of them so far as we know cared to sketch this man Jesus. There were many professional Jewish writers living in Jesus' day, but so far as we know not one of them took the trouble to write the story of Jesus' life. This is remarkable! To be sure, there are apocryphal gospels and apocryphal acts and apocryphal epistles and apocalypses, but no one of these, nor do all of them together, throw any light on the character of Jesus which is not furnished by our New Testament. Everything that is positively known of Jesus of Nazareth is confined between the covers of the New Testament. For years men have been ransacking the libraries, digging up the ruins of ancient cities, and delving into the desert sands thinking that possibly a page might be found that would throw additional light upon this Man. Seven years ago two Englishmen, digging in the sands of Middle Egypt, brought up two leaves of papyrus, one of them torn in two. A thrill of delight ran through the world of Christian scholarship at the thought that some new light might be thrown on Jesus' life. Alas! the new papyrus has nothing new to tell. The whole story must be sought within the narrow compass of the New Testament. But we can bring down the limits to a still narrower area. You can write the life of Jesus from the Book of the Acts, but it is a meagre life and contains practically nothing not to be found in the Gospels. You may also piece out a life of Jesus from the epistles of the New Testament, but the life is exceedingly defective and nothing of importance is added to the things already told in the Gospels. And therefore, so far as our present purpose is concerned, we may throw away all the other books of the New Testament and affirm that all which is known of the character of Jesus must be sought for inside the four Gospels. That the life of the greatest and most important man who ever lived upon the earth should be written on pages so small and few is one of the surprises.

When we study these Gospels we are surprised that they tell us so little, they do not give us a complete life of Jesus. They do not tell us how long Jesus lived, but from scattered hints it would seem that he lived something like thirty-three years. Thirty of these years are passed over with scarcely a word. They are deep sunken in a darkness into which no rays of light enter. The men who wrote the four Gospels did not attempt to deal with ten-elevenths of the life of Jesus. They simply let the larger part alone. Nor did they attempt to deal even with all the three years of his public ministry. They mention what he did or said only on from thirty to thirty-five days. That is, they confine their attention to one thirtieth of his public life, twenty-nine thirtieths being a total blank. Or, in other words, if he lived thirty-three years and the evangelists deal with only thirty-five days, they limit themselves to one three-hundredth part of his earthly career, and allow two hundred and ninety-nine three-hundredths to lie hidden. These men have recorded many things which he said, but his recorded sayings can be spoken easily within five hours. They tell many things which he did, but nearly all of them might have been crowded into a day, so meagre is their report of what Jesus said and did. It is evident, then, that we do not have as much information as we want. The question is. Do we have as much as we need? There is always a wide gap between what we want and what we need, and we need not be surprised that there is a gap here. These Gospels attempt to give us nothing but his words. They do not give us his facial expression, the quiver of the lip, the glance of the eye. We cannot see his smile or his frown. Facial expression is a revelation, and that revelation is lost forever. Nor do the evangelists attempt to give us his gestures. Gestures are interpreters of thought. A speaker speaks with his head, his shoulders, his hands, and by means of these gestures the thought is unfolded and made clear. Gesture is a revelation, and it is a revelation which has been lost forever. The New Testament does not give us the voice of Jesus. The voice is the best of all interpreters. By its modulations and cadences, by its inflexions and emphases, it reveals and explains and illustrates. The music of speech lies in the inflections, and many a word takes on a new glory from the way in which it is spoken. Intonation is a revelation, but in the case of Jesus it is a revelation which has been lost forever. And then there is another revelation to which we are denied access: the revelation of his sighs and his tears. We cannot see the tears on his cheeks as he looks down on Jerusalem and sobs, "O!" If we could have heard him weeping in the garden, we could have seen down deeper into his heart. But this revelation is denied us forever. We have nothing but words to deal with, and words are sometimes opaque and ambiguous, stumbling interpreters of the heart. But words are all that God has given us, and with words therefore we must be content.

Right here there springs up a new surprise: we are not to deal with Jesus' words. He spoke in i Aramaic, and there are not a dozen Aramaic words [left in the Gospels. He said to the little girl, "Talitha cumi," which being interpreted means, "Damsel, arise!" On the cross he said, "Eli, Eli, lama sabachthani?" which being interpreted means, "My God, my God, why hast thou forsaken me?" Besides these only an occasional Aramaic word has been recorded for us, and with these slight exceptions all the words that dropped from his lips have passed completely away. We read the English New Testament. Its words are not Jesus' words, they are the translators' words, the words chosen by scholars who have interpreted for us the Greek text. But even the Greek words were not spoken by Jesus, the Greek words were translators' words chosen to interpret the meaning of the Aramaic words. It is not unlikely there were Aramaic Gospels before the Greek Gospels were written. But the Aramaic Gospels have long since fallen to dust, and so also have the Greek Gospels. The first Greek copies were written on papyrus, and the papyrus was so frail and fragile that it perished probably in less than a hundred years. We have no copies of the New Testament that run back beyond the fourth century — and this also is a surprise.

Looking, then, at these words with which we have to deal, will they tell us anything of the personal appearance of the Nazarene? Nothing. The men who wrote the Gospels were not interested in the stature of Jesus, in the color of his eyes or hair, in the expression of his face, or the build of his body. The New Testament has been often scrutinized by men eager to get some hint of Jesus' personal appearance, but no such hint has been forthcoming. Expressions here and there have been seized upon and put upon the rack and tortured, in order to compel them to give at least a suggestion as to what Jesus looked like. But under torture every sentence of the Gospels remains absolutely silent on this most interesting question. We must therefore at the very beginning banish all pictures of Jesus from our minds. We do not know what he looked like. The artists have not known, they have simply painted from their own imagination. When an Italian paints the face of Jesus he puts a little of the Italian into it, when a German paints him he paints a little of the German into it, when a Spaniard paints him he paints a little of the Spaniard into it. That accounts also for the variety of the Madonnas. Raphael paints her as a lovely Italian girl, Murillo paints her as an innocent Spanish maiden, Sichel paints her as a German peasant girl. No artist can overcome completely the predilections of his own nationality. The artists then have simply painted their ideal, and their ideal is the creation of their own heart, and that is what you and I have a right to do. Would you conceive of Jesus as he appeared in the days of his flesh, you must form him according to your own ideal. You have the same right the artists have. This, then, is to be remembered, that we are not to study the personal appearance of Jesus, but the stamp of his mind and the bent of his spirit. In other words, we are to study his character.

But while the smiles and frowns, the intonations and modulations, the glance of the eye and the gesture of the hand, have all been lost and lost forever, we must not think that they were unimportant in the history of the world. All those things helped to make an impression on the men that stood nearest to Jesus. They saw his smile, caught the expression of his eye, heard him laugh, sigh, sob, drank in the music of his voice — and the question is, How were they affected? The New Testament tells us they were affected in two distinct and opposite ways. Some men were repelled. They disliked him, feared, hated, detested, loathed him. Their loathing became so venomous that they murdered him. They could not allow him to remain upon this earth. That is the effect which he produced upon one type of mind. There were other men who were attracted by him, they liked him, loved, adored, worshipped him, they were ready to die for him. It should never be forgotten that every one of his disciples, with one exception, laid down his life for Jesus, and that, too, after Jesus was dead. The men who were the nearest to him loved him with an adoration which was boundless, and they communicated the impression to other men, and the impression has come down to this present hour, so that at the beginning of the twentieth century thousands of miles from Palestine men are building churches in the name of Jesus, believing that his name is above every name, and that every knee should bow to him.

At the very beginning then of our study of the character of Jesus let us remember that Christianity is rooted in a life that was lived upon the earth. There is one part of the Christian creed which every human being can repeat without question and without reservation. There are men who might refuse to repeat the first article, "I believe in God the Father Almighty, Maker of heaven and earth." God is spirit, and a man might refuse to acknowledge that He exists. There are those who might stumble at the last clause in the creed, "I believe in the life everlasting." That also reaches out beyond the sweep of human sight, and there are men who will not affirm beyond that which they can see. But at the very centre of the creed there is one little paragraph to which no one can offer reasonable objection, "Suffered under Pontius Pilate, was crucified, dead, and buried." There are some who object to the supernatural, they do not like the extraordinary. Very well, let them begin with the ordinary, let them take their stand on the natural. Some of you may think that Christianity is in the air. Its branches, to be sure, are in the air, but its roots are in the earth. Its base is not in philosophy but in human history, not in poetry but in mundane experience. All that you see of Christianity in the world to-day came out of this man who lived in Palestine, who suffered under Pontius Pilate, was crucified, dead, and buried.

May I make of you this one request, — that while you follow my words you read St. Mark's Gospel from beginning to end. It is probably the oldest of all the Gospels, the shortest of them all, the most graphic of them all, and seems to come the nearest to Jesus as men saw him in the days of his humiliation. If you will read this Gospel, you will more easily follow me in these studies, and come to know better the one supreme character of history. It is a sad mistake for any man or any woman to leave religious matters entirely to the minister. The Roman Catholic who leaves everything to the priest does not grow in grace and in the knowledge of Jesus Christ our Lord. The Protestant who simply comes to church and listens to the preacher speak, and who makes no earnest effort to study for himself the great literature in which are enshrined the oracles of God — that Protestant fritters away his opportunities and does not build up within himself those deep convictions and that enduring knowledge which will make him a power and blessing in his day and generation. In other words, I cannot study the character of Jesus for you, you must study it for yourselves. All that I can hope to do is to drop suggestions which may possibly assist you in your study.

IV: THE STRENGTH OF JESUS

"And they were all amazed." — Mark i: 27.

We have seen that all the authentic materials for a Life of Christ are to be found in the four Gospels. When we study this material it turns out to be fragmentary and scanty. The writers deal with only three years out of thirty-three, and tell us of less than forty days out of three years, and of these selected days they deal only with shreds and fractions. Possibly somebody may say we cannot write a life of Jesus at all, and that is true, if by life of Jesus you mean a complete biography. But what if it should happen that the men who wrote the Gospels were not trying to write a biography of Jesus, but had something entirely different in mind. When Morley wrote the "Life of Gladstone" he filled three ponderous volumes. When Carlyle wrote the "Life of Frederick the Great" he wrote over six thousand pages, filling twenty-one books. When Nicolay and Hay wrote the "Life of Lincoln" they filled ten good-sized volumes. These Gospel writers evidently did not intend to write a biography of Jesus, otherwise they would not have confined themselves within such narrow limits. We are driven to the conclusion that they were writing not the biography of Jesus but the character of Jesus. A vast amount of material is necessary for a biography, but only a little material is needed for the elucidation of a character. You do not need all the words a man speaks, just a few of them will answer — every word is a flash of lightning, and like a flash of lightning lights up the world from horizon to horizon. You do not need many deeds, every deed is like a sunbeam touching a dark world into visibility. Notwithstanding the Gospels are so small, we know Jesus, his mind and heart and spirit, better than we know any other man who has ever lived upon the earth. Men who study the New Testament carefully feel that they know Jesus of Nazareth better than any other character of history. Some one may say, "Ah, Jesus lived two thousand years ago, and therefore we cannot be sure what his character really was." You are mistaken. You can understand a great man better at a distance than when standing near him. No truly great man is ever appreciated at his worth by the people in the midst of whom he lives. The world did not appreciate Abraham

Lincoln until he died. His great figure has been looming higher each succeeding decade, and the generations yet to come will understand him better than we do. We understand Luther far better than his contemporaries. We understand the apostles better than the fathers did. We understand Jesus of Nazareth better than has any other generation of men that has ever lived. A great man is like a mountain, you cannot appreciate it when standing at its base. You must throw miles between your eye and it before you can catch the symmetry of its sides and feel the majesty of its colossal dimensions. Just so it is with Jesus. Each succeeding generation will understand him better. He was so great that the men of Palestine could not take his measure. We are far better able to judge how great he was because we can see the length of the luminous shadow which he has cast across nineteen centuries and we can measure the volume of the stream which has flowed from the fountains of his heart. When you wish that you had lived in Jesus' day, you are wishing for a great misfortune. Had you lived in the first century you would most likely have been found among those who saw in Jesus nothing but a disturber of the peace. It may be that you would have joined the crowd that cried, "Crucify him!"

Let us look at Jesus across the distance of nineteen hundred years. When you picture him, what sort of face is it that stands out before you? That will depend upon the painting with which you are most familiar, or it will depend upon instruction which you have received from teachers, or it will depend upon the working of your own fancy or imagination. We instinctively begin to form the image of a person whom we have never seen, at the mere mention of his name. You have all tried it again and again. The fame of some great man has reached your ears, and your mind has gone to work at once and conceived what sort of man he is. Later on, it may be your eyes have looked upon him and you have said, "I was altogether mistaken in the image I had formed." It may be, therefore, that you have been misled by the painters, deceived by your teachers, led astray by your own imagination. It will be better to do away with all such images and try to see Jesus as men saw him who touched him in Judea and Galilee. Those were the men who heard his voice, saw the light in his eye, caught the expression of his face — they are the best witnesses therefore of what sort of a man he really was, and therefore we shall not listen to anything which Jesus himself said, we shall pay attention simply to the impression which he made upon the people. He was not a hermit or recluse, he pressed his life close to the lives of men, and therefore we have abundant material with which to deal in trying to find out what impression he made upon the people of his time.

What was the first impression which Jesus made upon his contemporaries? What has been his first impression on you? Has he impressed you as subdued and meek, calm and effeminate? Have you seen him always as many a painter has painted him, pale and ghastly, sickly, emaciated? When you think of him do you think of some one thin and gaunt, weak and pallid? Not so did he seem to the people of his day. Open the Gospel according to St. Mark. In the very first chapter he tells you in four different places what impression Jesus made upon men. He first tells you of the impression he made on John the Baptist. John the Baptist was a mighty man, none mightier had ever appeared in Judea; but John said there is coming one mightier than I. When Jesus presents himself to be baptized, a remarkable thing happens. John had called men to repentance, he had faced the greatest men of his day without flinching, he had baptized the great and small, the high and low, the rich and poor, the learned and ignorant; but when this man from Nazareth appears, John falters and draws back and says: "I cannot baptize you. I have need to be baptized by you." Such was the impression which Jesus made upon the intrepid reformer from the desert.

Let us take another illustration: He walks one day along the shore of the Sea of Galilee and sees two men fishing; he says, "Follow me," and straightway they left their nets and followed him. A few steps farther on he sees two other men, he says to them, "Follow me," and they left all and followed him. Such was the impression he made upon them. He goes into the synagogue and begins to teach, and they are amazed, not at what he says, but the manner in which he says it. He teaches them as one having authority and not as the scribes. There is something in his voice that pierces and cuts and thrills, a tone that they have never heard before. It is the note of authority, the note of strength. Or take another illustration: There is a sick man in the synagogue, and Jesus heals him, and again the people are surprised because God has given such power to a man. In these four instances the first impression of Jesus is the impression of authority, mastery, power, leadership; he is a man of strength. And that, I think, is the teaching of all the Gospels: they give us repeated illustrations of the power of Jesus. He drew men to him. Wherever he went he was surrounded by a crowd. He goes down to the seashore, and the crowd is so great they push him into the water and he gets into a boat. He goes to the hilltop, and immediately the hillside is alive with people. He goes to the desert, and immediately a great crowd surrounds him. Sometimes he dares not go into the city because of the tumult which his entrance will certainly stir up. Every city through which he passes is turned upside down by his presence. Only a man of strength draws to him great masses of men. It is noteworthy that widely differing classes of men are drawn: the publicans and sinners, the great unwashed crowd, they are drawn, but Nicodemus, a member of the supreme court of Palestine, he also is attracted, and the Roman centurion, he also is drawn, saying to Jesus; "I know what it is to command and so do you. There is an enemy in my house which I cannot order out, you speak the word and he will depart." Not only did Jesus draw men to him but he stirred them whenever they came near him. Have you ever noted how many times the evangelists say in speaking of the people: "they were astonished" — "they were astonished with a great astonishment" — "they were amazed" — "they were filled with amazement" — "they marveled"? The evangelists never say such things of themselves. Matthew never says, "I was surprised." Mark never says, "I was amazed." John never says, "I marvelled." They write all of them with an arm of marble; there is no feeling in the fingers that hold the pen; they simply write in cold blood the effect which Jesus had on others.

Probably no better illustration of the power of Jesus can be found than that which is afforded in the estimate which different classes of people put upon him. One day when Jesus propounded the question, "Who do men say that I am?" the disciples told him that men had different opinions in regard to him. Some said he was John the Baptist, some said he was Elijah, others said he was Jeremiah, while others unable to give his exact name felt convinced he was one of the old prophets. This is remarkable! They went to the grave in order to find a man to whom they could liken him. There was no man then living with whom he could be compared. We do the same thing. When we want to stir men's hearts, we appeal to the dead; when we search for the great, we descend into the grave, we talk of Shakespeare and Caesar, of Charlemagne and Alfred the Great, of Lincoln and Webster, we dare not use the name of a man living. That is what the Jews did. The name of no man living was great enough to convey their idea of the strength which they felt resided in Jesus. He was one of the giants of bygone ages who had come back to the earth carrying with him powers augmented by his sojourn in the realms of death. This tells us clearly that to them he was a man of tremendous power.

And if the Jews felt this in regard to him, what was the impression which he made upon the Roman officials? He impressed them in the same way. When the policemen came to arrest him and asked him if he was indeed Jesus of Nazareth, he turned upon them and simply said, "I am," and they fell backward to the ground. What do you suppose his eyes looked like that night when they outflashed the Roman torches and outshone the Syrian stars? Pilate is afraid of him. He is the representative of Caesar in Palestine. He is clothed with authority. Jesus is nothing but a poor unarmed peasant. Nevertheless Pilate is afraid of him, he draws back from him, he wrings his hands in uncertainty, he washes his hands, he tries to get rid of this man. He feels that there is a power in him unlike any power he has ever come in contact with before. But if you would have the finest proof of his power, you can find it in the intensity of the hatred and in the intensity of the love which he excited. How many hated him! They could not hear him talk without sizzling, hissing and boiling like a pot under which the fire roars. He stirred tempests in the heart, he awoke serpents in men. He drove them to madness until they cried out in frenzy, "Crucify him!" Only a great man can do that. You cannot hate a pygmy, a weakling, a ninny. You can hate Nero or Napoleon or any giant, but you cannot hate a nobody. Who was the most detested man in England during the last century? William E. Gladstone. We in America have little conception of the venomous hatred that was poured out upon that man. He stirred men to hatred because he was so mighty. Who are the men most detested in America to-day? Every one of them a man of tremendous power. The men that are loathed and feared are men of genius, who have in them extraordinary capacity for bringing things to pass.

But if Jesus drove some men to hate him, he drove other men to love him. He kindled a devotion that is superior to anything that has ever been known in this world. He kindled a fire which ran all over Palestine, and then around the edges of the Mediterranean, and then into the German forests, it then leaped over the English Channel, and later on it leaped over the Atlantic Ocean, and now it has leaped over all the oceans and is burning more brightly to-day than ever. And all this conflagration was kindled by his hot heart. These torches which are burning now have been carried down through the blasts of nineteen stormful centuries, and they have never gone out, because he lighted them. He called forth a kind of reverence that has never been granted to any other man who has ever lived. He was so mighty that when men thought of him, they thought of God. The man who stood the nearest to him saw him in a vision after he was gone, and he says, "When I saw him I fell at his feet as one dead."

V: THE SINCERITY OF JESUS

"Ye shall not be as the hypocrites."
— Matthew vi: 5.

All the graces are beautiful, but some have a finer loveliness than do others. All virtues are important, but some are more essential than others. There are virtues whose absence leaves the character ragged and marred, and there are others whose absence leaves the soul a hollow shell. Certain virtues are conspicuously ornamental, whereas others are plainly fundamental. If the former are not developed, the edifice is not complete; but if the latter are not present, the whole structure comes tumbling down in ruin. Such a fundamental virtue is the virtue of sincerity. It is the keystone in the arch without which the arch collapses. Or to change the figure it is the mother of a noble family of virtues, all of which draw their strength and beauty from it. Truthfulness, honesty, plainness, frankness, simplicity, these and many others are only children of the Queen — Sincerity.

It is the virtue which the human heart instinctively craves and looks for. It is a trait which a parent's eyes seek for in his children. Anything like deceit or trickery or sham in a child causes the parental heart to bleed. "Do you mean what you are saying?" "Are you telling me what you really feel?" "Are you concealing from me things which I ought to know?" There is nothing which a parent desires so much in his children as the unaffected simplicity of a sincere heart. This is what we demand in all the higher relationships of life. In the lower relationships sincerity is desirable, but in the higher ones it is absolutely indispensable. A man may sweep the pavement or make our garden, and do both well even though he is at heart a cheat. But we like him better and we feel more comfortable in his presence if he looks up at us out of honest eyes. A servant may hold his place and be insincere, not so a friend. There is an adjective which the word "friend" will not keep company with, and that is the adjective "insincere." You cannot induce them to stay together in the same room. They flatly contradict each other. The moment we find out that a comrade is insincere with us, he ceases to be our friend. Sincerity is the very blood and breath of friendship. "Pure gold he is," we say with exultation, meaning that in our friend there is no alloy. His nature is unspoiled and unadulterated. We can rely upon him through the twenty-four hours of every day. We are so constructed that we look for sincerity in others, and when we do not find it we are grieved and disappointed. When what we have taken for sincerity turns out to be nothing but an imitation, our heart sinks within us and we feel like a man who has been stabbed. There is nothing which so takes the life out of us as the discovery that some one whom we have trusted has been other than what he seemed to be. The very suspicion that some one whose life is close to us is insincere renders us restless and makes the universe seem insecure.

And yet how common insincerity is. What a miserable old humbug of a world we are living in, full of trickery and dishonesty and deceit of every kind. Society is cursed with affectation, business is honeycombed with dishonesty, the political world abounds in duplicity and chicanery, there is sham and pretence and humbuggery everywhere. Some use big words they do not understand, and some lay claim to knowledge which they do not have, and some parade in dresses which they cannot pay for; the life of many a man and many a woman is one colossal lie. We say things which we do not mean, express emotions which we do not feel, we praise when we secretly condemn, we smile when there is a frown on the face of the heart, we give compliments when we are really thinking curses, striving a hundred times a week to make people think we are other than we are. It is a penitentiary offence to obtain money under false pretences, and so from this we carefully refrain. But how many other things are obtained, do you think, by shamming and pretending, for which there is no penalty but the condemnation of Almighty God? Yes, it is a sad, deceitful, demoralized world in the midst of which we find ourselves; but thank God there are hearts here and there upon which we can evermore depend. We have tested them and we know them to be true. Life would not be worth the living if there were no one on earth sincere. It is to the honest heart that we return again and again, seeking rest and finding it. It is a fountain at which we drink and refresh ourselves for the toilsome journey. Beautiful, indeed, is the virtue of sincerity. It is not a gaudy virtue. It does not glitter. It has no sparkle in it. But it is substantial. It is life giving. It sustains and nourishes the heart. It is a virtue within the reach of the humblest of us. There are some things we cannot be, and many things which we cannot do. But this one thing is within the reach of us all, — we may pray God unceasingly to keep our heart sincere.

Would you see sincerity in its loveliest form, then come to Jesus. Here is a man incapable of a lie. Nothing was so abhorrent to him as falsehood. No other people so stirred his wrath as men who pretended to be what they were not. The most odious word upon his lips was the word "hypocrite." Have you ever wondered why it is impossible to speak that word without it falling from the lips like a serpent — it is because his curse is resting on it. It was not a harsh word before he spoke it, but he breathed the hot breath of his scorn into it, and it has been ever since a word degraded and lost. A hypocrite is an actor. It is a word taken originally from the stage. In the theatre we expect men and women to be other than they seem to be. An ordinary plebeian wraps round him the robes of a king, talks like a king, and acts like one, and we are not offended, because we are not deceived. It is expected that on the stage no one shall seem to be what he really is. But on the great stage of the world God expects every man to be what he claims to be. If we say things we do not believe, and profess things we do not feel, and lay claim to things which we do not possess, we are tricksters and deceivers, causing mischief and confusion in the world. It was the sincerity of Jesus which drove him into deadly conflict with the hypocrites. A hypocrite and Jesus cannot live together.

It was his constant exhortation that men should speak the truth. The religious leaders of his day had divided oaths into two classes, — one class binding, the other not. If an oath contained the name of God, it was binding on the conscience; if for God's name some other name was substituted, then the conscience might go free. Jesus was disgusted by the reasoning of the bat-eyed pettifoggers. "Do not swear at all," he said. "Let your communication be yea, yea, nay, nay." In other words, "If you want to render a thing emphatic, simply say it over again. If men doubt you, then quietly repeat what you have already declared." It was the belief of Jesus that a man's word ought to be as good as his oath, or as we say as good as his bond. If the world were the kind of world God wants it to be, then all the evidence that would be needed to prove a certain thing true would be that a man had asserted it. If it is necessary now in courts of justice to make use of oaths, that is because of the Evil One who has corrupted many hearts and rendered the ordinary speech of humanity unreliable. In an ideal world all oaths are unnecessary and unthought of.

It was because of Jesus' incorruptible sincerity that we have from his lips such a remarkable outpouring of plain words. You and I do not like plain words. We dare not use them — at least often. We water our words down. We pull the string out of them. We substitute long Latin words for plain, short, Anglo-Saxon words, for by multiplying the syllables we attenuate the meaning. For instance, we say "prevarication" instead of "lie," because falsehood when expressed pompously loses its blackness and grossness. But Jesus would not use words of velvet when words of velvet flattered and deceived. It was his work to help men see themselves as they were. He characterized them by words which accurately described their character. One day he told a crowd in the city of Jerusalem that they were of their father the devil, and that the lusts of their father they were eager to do. He went on to add that the devil was a murderer and that he abode not in the truth because the truth was not in him. We are shocked by such plainness of speech. We do not like it. Is that because we dare not express things as they are? Have we gotten into the habit of hiding our eyes and trying to make black things seem gray or even white?

Jesus was incorrigibly sincere, and it was sincerity which drove him to tell men the plain truth. He said to these men, "If I should say I do not know God, I should be a liar like you." There was a strong inducement for him to conceal his extraordinary knowledge. A man makes himself odious by claiming to know more than other men, and by asserting that he can do more than anybody else. It would have been easier for Jesus to adopt the language of the professionally humble people who are always saying that they do not know anything and cannot do anything and do not amount to anything. But Jesus was a man of truth. He could not disguise the fact that his knowledge was unique and that his power was unparalleled. Because he was true he could not hold back the fact that he was the Good Shepherd and the Door, the Bread of Life, and the Light of the World. Nothing but sincerity would ever have driven him to outrage the feelings of his countrymen by assertions so extraordinary. Had he kept silence or pretended to be ignorant on matters on which he possessed full knowledge, he would indeed have been a liar like the very men with whom he was struggling. All these remarkable declarations of his in regard to the nature of his personality and the range of his power were forced from his lips by a heart unswervingly loyal to the truth.

The warnings of Jesus have often aroused criticism and condemnation because of their severity and the frightening words in which they are expressed. He told certain men they were moving onward to perdition and painted their loss and ruin in phrases which have caused the human heart to shudder. How will you account for such vigor of language? It was certainly cruel to speak such words if he did not know the possibilities and doom of sin. If he knew, then he was bound to tell. The awful parables of the New Testament are the product of a heart that was uncompromisingly sincere. To speak soft words to men whose feet are hastening down the road to ruin, how was it possible to do it? His very sincerity drove him into language which to our cold hearts seems exaggerated and needlessly abusive. He called the leaders in Jerusalem liars, blind men, fools, serpents, vipers. If they were not all this, then Jesus stands condemned for making use of such cutting words. But suppose these men were precisely what such words described — then what? Suppose they were in very fact liars and fools and blind men, was it not the duty of Jesus to inform them of their pitiable condition? What else could a sincere friend do? These men supposed they could see and were wise, but if they were mistaken was it not incumbent on an honest man to deliver them if possible from their delusion? If they were venomous, and deadly and treacherous, why should they not be likened to serpents and vipers? There is not a trace of bitterness in Jesus' language. It is the calm statement of a horrible fact. The Lord of truth must of necessity use words which accurately characterize the persons who are to be instructed and warned.

The inmost heart of Jesus finds utterance in his declaration to Pontius Pilate that he had come into the world to bear witness to the truth. That was his work. He never shirked it. He never grew weary in doing it. He was surrounded all his life by men who bore witness to falsehoods. They lied about him in every city in which he worked. They misrepresented his deeds and his words and his motives. They filled all the air with lies. The witnesses who appeared against him at his trial were liars. But in the midst of the despicable set of false-minded, false-hearted maligners, and murderers he stood forth, calm, radiant, the one man in all the world whose lips had never been sullied by a falsehood and whose heart had never been stained by a lie.

In the centuries which have passed since Jesus died, many strange and uncomplimentary things have been said about him; but it is surprising how loath men have been to accuse him of deceit. They have been willing to say he was mistaken, they have called him a visionary, a fanatic, an enthusiast, and dreamer; but no man of sane mind or heart has ever ventured to assert that Jesus of Nazareth was an intentional deceiver. Men have claimed that his apostles were rogues and falsifiers, that they deliberately misrepresented both his person and his teaching; but no one has dared to argue that Jesus himself was capable of a lie. There is something so pure and frank and noble about him that to doubt his sincerity would be like doubting the brightness of the sun.

This unquestioned loyalty to truth gives his words a value which no other words possess. When we listen to the words of other men, we must make subtractions and allowances. No man puts his whole self into his speech. His words reveal him and they also conceal him. There is a discrepancy between the soul and what the mouth declares. Not so with Jesus. He holds back nothing. What he thinks he says, what he feels he declares. He tones down nothing, he exaggerates nothing. He declares all things as they are. He is not swerved by sin within nor cowed by hostile forces from without. His character is revealed in his speech. A Chinese proverb says that words are the sounds of the heart. This is certainly true of the words of Jesus. His words are simply the pulsations of his heart. They are unlike any other words ever spoken. They contain the full-statured spirit of a man. In these words his great soul comes out and stands before us, and in them we behold his glory.

This, then, is the man we want. A man like this can be a refuge in the time of storm. To him we can flee; when sick at heart, because of the deceptions of the world, we cry out in wretchedness, "Who shall show us any good?" When men disappoint us and friends are few, we can come to one who says, "I am the truth." When we are weary and heavy laden, we can rest our souls upon one who is as certain as the morning and as faithful as the stars. The world is filled with jangling voices and it is hard to know which voice to trust; but his voice has in it something which inspires assurance and quenches uncertainty and doubt. What he teaches about God we can receive. What he says of the soul we can believe. What he declares of sin and the penalty of sin we can accept. What he tells us of the soul we can depend upon. What he asserts concerning the principles of a victorious life we can act upon, never doubting. When he tells us to do a thing we can do it, assured that that is the best thing to do. When he warns us against a course of action we can shun it, knowing that in that direction lie night and death. The path which he exhorts us all to take we can take with boldness, convinced that if we take it we shall arrive safe at home at last. When he says that him that cometh unto him he will in no wise cast off, we are certain that if we come we shall be received. When he says, "Behold I stand at the door and knock; if any man will hear my voice and open the door I will come in and sup with him and he with me," we are certain of a heavenly guest if we want him. This, then, is why we feel so calm and satisfied with Jesus: he soothes and heals us by being genuine. The heart is always at peace when it rests upon a heart which is sincere.

VI : THE REASONABLENESS OF JESUS

"In the beginning was the logos."
— John i: 1.

Let us think of the reasonableness of Jesus, of his sanity, his level headedness, his common sense, his soundness of mind. An illustrious Roman poet was convinced that man's supreme prayer ought to be for a sound mind in a healthy body. A sound mind in a sound body has been the summum bonum aimed at by all the great systems of education both ancient and modern. The ideal was realized in Jesus of Nazareth. Unsoundness of mind is far more common than is ordinarily supposed. The mind altogether sane is rare, and there are those who declare that it is never found at all. The men and women imprisoned in insane asylums are only a fraction of the host of mortals whose mental operations are deranged. Our very language bears pathetic witness to the wide range of mental disturbance. Do we not speak of the crack-brained and of the scatter-brained, and of people who are daft? There are crotchety brains and freakish brains, eccentric and erratic brains, capricious, whimsical, and hysterical brains, unhinged and unbalanced brains of many types and grades, and when a man has a mind which works normally and sanely, we pay him the compliment of declaring him to be a man of common sense. We call it "common" sense not because it is prevalent, but because it is a combination of the qualities and forces which, scattered among many individuals, may be said to belong to the common race of men. Jesus was a man of unparalleled common sense.

Would you see how rational he is, study his attitude to life. There is a widespread impression, especially among young people of a certain age, that Jesus is unreasonable, and that Christianity is a religion which constantly makes war on reason. Young men sometimes say, "I do not want to join the church because I want to use my reason." How strange such language when Jesus from first to last pleads for the use of the reason. Christianity is the one religion of the world which demands the continuous and daring exercise of the intellect. Men often think they are using their reason when in fact they are exercising their prejudices or are suffering from paralysis of the brain. I have heard men rail at Christianity as unreasonable because a certain Christian man had said a certain thing, as though Jesus of Nazareth must be held responsible for everything that every follower of his may think or say. Other men have been hopelessly estranged from Christianity because of certain statements they have read in certain books. How unreasonable! It surely is not fair to hold Jesus of Nazareth responsible for everything which men who bear his name may think and publish. If men want to know whether Christianity is reasonable or not, why do they not read the Gospels? They are short and can be read through at least once a week, and yet men go right on refusing to read the Gospels — the one source of all authentic information as to what the Christian religion really is. Many think nothing of reading a novel of four hundred pages who stagger under the task of reading the four Gospels. It is just such persons who like to talk about the unreasonableness of Christianity. Why not be reasonable? Christianity has but one authoritative volume. Why not read it?

Open your New Testament, then, and see Jesus' attitude to life. The word "life" was often on his lips. He loved the thing and he therefore loved the word. He wanted men to live. The tragedy of the world to him was that human life was everywhere so thin and meagre. "I came that they may have life, and may have it more abundantly," thus did he express the object of his coming. "I am the resurrection and the life," "I am the way, and the truth, and the life." It was in such phrases that he endeavored to give men an idea of his mission and his person. Men everywhere want to live, but the tragedy of the world is that they do not succeed. There is a path which leads to life, but there are only a few who find it. Tennyson expressed what every heart feels in his lines: —

"'Tis life of which my nerves are scant,
More life and fuller that I want."

But, alas! we do the very things which curtail the capacity for living and dry up the springs of vitality. We are imitative creatures, all of us, and we mimic the habits and methods of those around us to our hurt. We are cowards all of us, and we allow ourselves to be hoodwinked and browbeaten and cheated out of our birthright. We are greedy, all of us, and in our eagerness to secure the things on which we have set our heart we become feverish and wretched, losing out of life its richest satisfactions. We are short-sighted, all of us, and in order to attain immediate ends we barter away the treasures of coming years. Life is not full or rich or sweet for many of us because we are handicapped by our doubts and hampered by our fears and enslaved by the unreasonable standards and requirements of a foolish world. It is the aim of Jesus to break the fetters and let life out to its completion. To do a thing which reduces the volume and richness of a man's life is foolish. We are reasonable in our conduct only when we are doing things which give life fuller capacity and power. Jesus was always reasoning with men in regard to the right way of living. Life to him was ever the treasure of transcendent importance, and his question, "What shall it profit a man if he gain the whole world and lose his life?" is one of the sentences which having once dropped into the world's mind are sure to stay forever.

In order to expose the folly of men, Jesus had the habit of asking questions. Foolishness can never be made ashamed of itself unless it is compelled to look into its own face. Men do stupid and silly things because they do not think. They would cease doing them if they would take time for reflection. Jesus was always saying, "What do you think?" His only hope for men is in getting them to think. His attitude from first to last is the attitude of God as pictured by Isaiah. He was always saying, "Come, now, let us reason together."

The Sermon on the Mount is the part of the New Testament which is nowadays universally praised, and no wonder. Every sentence is a pearl, and every paragraph is the classical expression of unadulterated common sense. How sane is his remark on the subject of profanity! Swearing was common in his day as it is also in our own. But profanity is always irrational and nonsensical, and this will be admitted even by those who indulge in it. The Hebrew had a deep-seated reverence for the name of God, and therefore he did not use God's name, but substituted the name of his city, or God's throne, or the earth, or the heavens, or his own head, all of which was puerile and absurd. And Jesus holds the practice up to scorn. Say what you want to say and then stop. "All superfluous words are both needless and mischievous." Is not this common sense? If a man wants to express a feeling or a thought, why does he drag in words which have no connection either with the thought or the feeling, and if he is expressing a feeling which is low and brutal, why should he pad his sentences with the most sacred names of religion? Profanity is a sin against reason. There is no sense in it. A man swears because he is weak, his vocabulary is limited, his power of self-control is stunted, his brain acts abnormally. Profanity is utterly senseless and ridiculous. A man who swears acts like a fool. The soul of Jesus revolted against it because it was so stupid and irrational.

It is this illumination of a mind altogether sane which he brings to the discussion of prayer. Men in the first century had overdeveloped the forms of prayer. The body had outgrown the soul. Men multiplied words but were poor in ideas and emotion. They said the same thing over and over again and called it praying. They repeated pious words on the street corners and were satisfied if their neighbors looking on called it praying. To Jesus all such devotion was ridiculous. If God is an intelligent Being, what is the use of any such mummery and mockery as this? If God is Spirit, then to pray to him is to come into communion with him, and you can do that best when you are alone and have shut all the world out. It is not necessary to multiply words, the things essential being sincerity and spiritual contact. How sensible, so reasonable that it will never become obsolete. Equally sane is he on the subject of fasting. The exercise of fasting in Palestine had been elaborated into a system. Men fasted by the clock. Precise rules were laid down and to obey these regulations punctiliously was the ambition of the pious. Men fasted not only once but several times every week, and all this was supposed to be pleasing to God. But to Jesus the whole system was mechanical and abominable. There was no reason in it. It was utterly formal and deadening and stupid. Moreover, to make a display of it and flaunt the signs of it in the eyes of the world was contemptible. Fasting if it is to have value at all must be an exercise of the soul. It is the spirit which is central and which must control. It is not the abstinence from food which is pleasing to the Almighty, but the condition of the heart of the person who is doing the fasting. Moreover, fasting cannot be done by the clock. Jesus refused to obey the rules of the Rabbis. He did not ask his disciples to obey them either. Many punctilious souls were sorely distressed. They came to Jesus for an explanation. His reply carried them to the very centre of the whole problem. "Can the sons of the bridechamber mourn as long as the bridegroom is with them? but the days will come when the bridegroom shall be taken away from them, and then will they fast." How illuminating and sensible! Fasting is a spiritual exercise. The body is to be controlled by the spirit. There are seasons when the soul is jubilant and then fasting is not in order; there are seasons when the soul is depressed, and at such times the body does not crave food. Fasting according to rule is irrational. Such fasting is not a part of the religion of Jesus, but wherever it exists in Christendom to-day it is merely a survival of Judaism.

Often Jesus illuminates an entire region of moral action by a question. Many a bubble of earthly vanity did he prick by the sharp point of a piercing interrogation. "Is not the life more than food?" Of course it is. Everybody knows that it is, the moment he stops to think about it. And yet thousands of mortals forget that life comes first, and by putting eating first they rob life of its glory. What a deal of fussing there is among people who are reputed sensible, about the dishes and the knives and the forks and the goblets and the number of courses! The simple act of eating is elaborated and made more and more ceremonious and complex until women break down under the burden, and life loses its zest and its joy. "Is not the body more than raiment?" Yes, it is, now that we stop to think about it; but it would seem, were we to judge from the conduct of a considerable part of the world, that the raiment is more than the body. Thousands fashion their lives upon the principle that the clothes are first and the body second. What the body needs in order that every organ in it may do easily and healthfully its appointed work, is in many cases not at all considered. Rather the question is: What is the fashion? What does the world of style demand? The clothes are hung up and the body is made to conform to the clothes, even though the body may be made to suffer in the operation and the volume of physical life be dangerously diminished. Who can number the people who are dragging out an existence pallid and nerveless, all because they have made the raiment of more moment than the body?

To the clear eye of Jesus all such conduct is insensate and wicked. Life comes first. Human beings must dress in ways which shall best conserve the physical resources of the body and make it easiest for the body to live the life which God has appointed it to live. That is reasonable, even though the whole world should deny it. His questions always pierce. "Is not a man better than a sheep?" Of course he is, even though the foolish world does not always act as though it believed it. In the first century men were far more solicitous about the well-being of their cattle than about the welfare of men who were not linked to them by ties of blood. This form of barbarism has not yet entirely passed away. A horse cannot fall in the street of any American city without men rushing at once to its assistance and getting it again on its feet. A horse down in the street is a sight intolerable. But a man down in the street dead drunk in some nook or corner is a sight which makes boys laugh, and even grown men pass by him without even so much as a thought of pity. Society is not yet reasonable in its treatment of animals and men.

Jesus would not allow himself to be swayed or daunted by institutions however sacred. Among the Jews there was no institution held in higher reverence than the Sabbath. So deep was the reverence that it degenerated into slavery. The day was made so holy that there was no living with it. The rules of Sabbath observance were so numerous that one could not turn round without breaking several of them. The reported discussions of the most sensible men in Palestine on Sabbath observance in the days of Jesus amaze us by their puerility and senselessness. Jesus saw at once through all the mass of rubbish which had accumulated round the subject, and laid down a maxim which shed light brilliant as the sun at noon. "The Sabbath was made for man and not man for the Sabbath." The life of man is the first thing to consider always. The day is the servant of the man. Is it lawful to do good on the Sabbath Day? Is it lawful to save life on the Sabbath? It was with such questions that he punctured the inflated reasonings of the Jerusalem dunces, and set men free from a bondage which had become intolerable. His view of Sabbath observance is reasonable.

But time would fail to deal with all the evidences of his matchless common sense. He put to flight a whole troop of simpletons by the quiet remark, "They that are whole have no need of a physician, but they that are sick." He asked men to do great things, but he always gave them a reason why they should follow his instructions. The foolish heart is always devising new objections to prayer, but he overthrows all the objections which have ever been offered or ever can be offered by his simple question: "What man is there of you, who, if his son shall ask him for a loaf, will give him a stone? or if he shall ask for a fish will give him a serpent? If ye then, being evil, know how to give good gifts unto your children, how much more shall your Father which is in heaven give good things to them that ask him?" To be sure! All that is best in us must be rooted in the deep heart of God. The fact that we love to give good things to our children is proof that that same disposition exists in the heart of the Eternal Father. We should never have had the disposition had he not had it first. If we give, of course He gives and will forever give. How reasonable! How unanswerable! All arguments against prayer are unreasonable. There is one sentence in the New Testament which by the vote of the world has been counted golden: "All things, therefore, whatsoever ye would that men should do unto you, even so do ye also unto them." What is this but perfect sense?

But some one may ask: Does not Christianity insist upon a namby-pamby attitude to the forces of the world? Does Jesus not virtually exhort his disciples to lie down and let men walk over them? No. You have gotten that idea from books other than the New Testament. Jesus is sensible at every point. "Give not that which is holy unto the dogs, neither cast your pearls before the swine, lest haply they trample them under their feet and turn and rend you." Who are the dogs? A certain kind of men. Who are the swine? Another type of men. We are to discriminate. All men are not alike. All men are not to be treated alike. There were men on whom Jesus turned his back. There were men whom Jesus refused to answer. The High Priest was amazed because he held his tongue. Pontius Pilate was enraged because his prisoner would not answer him. Here again we have common sense perfected. Some of us are foolish enough to think we must answer every dunce who chatters, reply to every question which is asked. Such is not our duty. When Jesus sent his disciples out to preach, he told them if people were unwilling to listen to them, to shake the dust from their sandals against them and go somewhere else. He followed that plan himself. No limp and sugary weakling was he. He faced men when necessary with a flash of indignation that frightened them and poured out upon them words which raised blisters. Nowhere is he more sensible than in his attitude to bad men.

But some one says, "Is he not unreasonable in demanding that we believe a lot of doctrines which we cannot understand?" Where does he demand that? Put your finger on the place, for I cannot find it. When I open the New Testament I hear him saying: "Follow me! Follow me!" That is his favorite exhortation. And when men wanted to know how they were to ascertain whether or not he was indeed a leader worthy of being followed, his reply was, "If any man willeth to do His will, he shall know of the teaching whether it be of God, or whether I speak from myself." Is this not reasonable? Jesus says if you want to understand the Christian life, then work at it. If you desire to know the truth, then live it. This is common sense. How else could one find the truth of a religion if he did not work at it? If you want to learn to speak Italian, you do not simply think about it, or read about it, but you go to work on it. It requires a deal of work, but no matter. You cannot learn a language without making mistakes, and the only thing to do is to keep on working. Just so is it with the Christian life. Men imagine they can become Christians by thinking about it, or by reading about it, or by hearing a preacher talk about it. How absurd! You can never become a Christian until you are willing to work at it. Are you willing to begin now?

VII: THE POISE OF JESUS

"No man after that durst ask him any question."
— Mark xii: 34.

By the poise of Jesus I mean the fine balance of his faculties, the equilibrium of his nature. Every boy knows what it is to balance a cane on his hand, or to poise a cane by resting one end of it on the tip of his finger. After a little practice it is possible for him to hold the cane absolutely erect. This equilibrium is a state of rest brought about by the counteraction of two or more opposing forces. Just so a man can poise himself in the midst of the storms of this boisterous world. This equilibrium is due first of all to a certain balance of faculty. How rarely do we find well-balanced men! The average man is one-sided, unsymmetrical, unevenly developed. When a man is unsymmetrical in his body, we pity him. If one arm is much longer than the other arm, or one leg is much shorter than the other leg, or one ear is much larger than the other ear, we say he is deformed, and his deformity calls forth our pity.

But this lack of symmetrical development in the body is nothing compared with the lack of symmetry in the mind. It is a rare thing to find a man or a woman deformed in his body; it is a rare thing not to find a man deformed in his spirit. We are all overdeveloped on one side of our nature and underdeveloped on the other. It seems to be well-nigh impossible to keep our faculties in even balance. If we are strong in certain characteristics, we are, well-nigh certain to be weak in the opposite characteristics. If we are enthusiastic, tremendously enthusiastic, our enthusiasm pushes ahead until it becomes fanaticism. If we are emotional, exceedingly emotional, our emotion degenerates into hysterics. If we are imaginative, very imaginative, unless we are on our guard we become flighty and visionary. If we are practical, very level-headed, we are always in danger of becoming prosaic and dull. If we have courage in great abundance, our courage passes readily into recklessness. If we are prudent, our prudence is always on the point of degenerating into cowardice. If we are original and unique, our uniqueness is always in danger of passing into eccentricity. If we are sympathetic, our sympathy is likely to run into sentimentalism. If we are pious, our piety has a tendency to become sanctimoniousness. If we are religious, our religion tends to slip into superstition. Every virtue when pushed beyond its appointed limit becomes a vice, and every grace when overdeveloped becomes a defect and disfiguration. Look around upon the men and women that you know, and in how many of them can you say that their disposition is finely balanced? "Oh, if he did not have so much of that!" "Oh, if he only had a little more of this!" That is what we always feel when the characters of men pass before us for judgment." He would be an ideal man — but —," "She would be a queen among women — but —." There is always just a little something lacking to make the character what it ought to be.

But when we come to Jesus we find ourselves in the presence of a man without a flaw. He was enthusiastic, blazing with enthusiasm, but he never became fanatical. He was emotional, men could feel the throbbing of his heart, but he never became hysterical. He was imaginative, full of poetry and music, seeing pictures everywhere, throwing upon everything he touched a light that never was on land or sea, the inspiration and the poet's dream — but he was never flighty. He was practical, hard-headed, matter of fact, but he was never prosaic, never dull. His life always had in it the glamour of romance. He was courageous but never reckless, prudent but never a coward, unique but not eccentric, sympathetic but never sentimental. Great streams of sympathy flowed from his tender heart toward those who needed sympathy, but at the same time streams of lava flowed from the same heart to scorch and overwhelm the workers of iniquity. He was pious, but there is not a trace about him of sanctimoniousness.

All the oily disgusting piety which has been caricatured in the books is the product of undeveloped hearts and minds far removed from the piety of his robust soul. He was religious, the most profoundly religious man that ever turned his face toward God, but never once did he slip into superstition. And because he is so well rounded and on every side so complete, men have never known where to class him. Of what temperament was he? It is impossible to say. Every man on coming to him finds in him what he wants. He had in him all the virtues, and not one of them was overgrown. He exhibited all the graces, and every one of them was in perfect bloom. He stands in history as the one man beautiful, symmetrical, absolutely perfect.

Out of this balance of his powers comes his unrivalled poise in conduct. He lived always in a whirlwind, — men bent like reeds around him, — he never so much as wavered. Men laid their traps and tried to catch him, he walked bravely in the midst of them and never was entrapped. The intellectual athletes of his time tried to trip him — they never did. His enemies did their best to upset him — they never could. They flung their lassos at his head — they never got a lasso round his neck. They dug their pits — he never tumbled into them. Wherever he went he was surrounded by enemies waiting to catch him in his talk — they never caught him. They asked him all sorts of questions, expecting that by his answers he would incriminate himself — he never did. They brought out to him one dilemma after another, saying we will catch him on one horn or the other — but he escaped them every time. After they had done their best they retired vanquished from the field. He remained undisputed conqueror.

This wonderful poise came out in the temple when he was only a boy of twelve. The old men in the midst of whom he sat were astounded at his answers. At the beginning of his public career he heard the seductive voices sounding in his ears. Time and again the evil one came to him with a new allurement, but every time he hurled the tempter back by quoting just the passage of Scripture which that temptation needed. Men tried to convict him of breaking the law in regard to the Sabbath day, but instantly he proved from Scripture and from reason that what he did was right. Men interrupted him in the midst of his preaching, but he was never disconcerted. "Make my brother," cried a man, "divide the inheritance with me." And quick as a flash the answer came: "Who made me a ruler over you? Let me tell you and everybody else to beware of covetousness." When Peter at Philippi began to protest against his going to Jerusalem where he would be killed, Jesus said, "Get thee behind me, Satan." He had heard that voice before. He recognized it even on the lips of his friend. It is one of the devil's last resources to speak through the mouth of a friend. Such a trick cannot deceive Jesus.

On the last Tuesday of his life they determined to undo him. All the different parties united their forces and put their heads together and concocted schemes by means of which this young prophet should be brought to prison. The Pharisees go to him with this question: "Is it lawful to pay tribute to Caesar?" It was an insidious question. If he said "yes," then that would make him hateful to every patriotic Jew, for no Jew who had a patriotic heart believed it was right to pay Jewish money into a

Gentile treasury. If on the other hand he said "no," then he proved himself to be a traitor to Rome, and the Roman officials could immediately pounce down on him. What will he do? Holding a piece of money in his hands he says, "Whose superscription is this?" And when they say "Caesar's," he hands the money back to them, saying, "Render unto Caesar the things that are Caesar's, and unto God the things that are God's." The Pharisees were conceited people, but after that they durst ask him no more questions. There was a scribe who thought he would try his hand. "What is the great commandment of the law?" he said, to which Jesus replied, "Love the Lord thy God with all thy heart and thy neighbor as thyself." "But who is my neighbor?" And then Jesus told him about the priest and the Levite and the Samaritan who saw the man by the wayside. After he had told the story he thrust this question into the man's heart: "Which one of the three was neighbor to the man who fell among the robbers?" After that the scribes asked him no more questions. The time comes when he is seized and carried before Caiaphas, and the marvelous poise of the prophet disconcerts and dumfounds the high priest. Unable to do anything with him he sends him to Pilate. Pilate questions him and becomes afraid of him. What a picture! The prophet of Galilee erect, calm, immovable, saying, "To this purpose was I born, and for this end came I into the world, to bear witness to the truth." See Pilate cringing, cowering, shuffling, washing his hands and saying he does not propose to have anything to do with such a man. Jesus has poise, and Pilate, representative of the Eternal City, servant of an empire of blood and iron — has no poise at all. It is an interesting fact that notwithstanding Jesus was speaking constantly in public for three years, not one of his enemies was able to catch him in his speech, and when at last they convicted him they had to do it on a trumped-up lie.

This also is noteworthy that not one of the enemies of Jesus was able by unfairness or falsehood or hatred to push Jesus into a hasty word or an unrighteous mood. Most men are so poorly balanced you can push them with very little pressure into an unmanly speech, into an unchristian disposition. Jesus was so firmly poised that under the pressure of the most venomous vituperation that has ever been hurled against a man, he stood erect, unmoved, and unmovable. His poise was divine.

Because he is so well balanced and so finely poised, each succeeding generation comes back to him for inspiration. Is it not remarkable that the men of the first century thought they saw in him the ideal figure of what a man should be, and that men in the fourth century looking at him felt the same, and that men in the tenth century looking at him felt the same, and that men in the sixteenth century looking at him agreed with all the centuries that went before, and that men in the twentieth century looking at him feel that in him they find a perfect pattern? Men of intellect who live the intellectual life look to him for guidance and instruction, men of emotion who desire to replenish the springs of feeling look to him for inspiration, men of high aspirations who desire to lift the soul sit humbly at his feet confessing that he has the words of life. And now that new and complicated problems have arisen in commercial life, and industrial life, and social life, men are turning wistfully toward him, feeling that he has the key which will unlock all the doors, that he knows the secret of a complete and perfect life. There is a grace about him which does not fade, there is a sanity about him which compels respect, there is a charm about him which wooes and wins the heart, and we like preceding generations fall down before him acknowledging that his character is without a flaw and that his life is without a blemish.

VIII: THE ORIGINALITY OF JESUS

"I make all things new."
— Revelation xxi: 5.

The word "originality" does not occur in the New Testament, for no one in Palestine ever raised the question whether Jesus was original or not. Every one took it for granted that he was. Wherever he went the eyes of men opened wide. Judea had become a drowsy place, but Jesus by his teaching shook it out of its lethargy and sleep. Wherever he went men were stirred to fever heat by what they saw and by what they heard, and cried out in astonishment, "We have never seen it after this fashion." His teaching itself struck Jesus' contemporaries as novel. "A new teaching!" was the exclamation which followed many of his discourses. It was the opinion of his severest critics that no man had ever spoken as he was speaking. There was something in the manner as well as in the matter which arrested attention and threw a fresh light upon God and men. There had been many a teacher in Palestine, but not one of his predecessors had spoken with his accent. The common people observed at once that his manner was not the manner of the professional teacher of the land. He taught them as one who possessed authority. The man himself, men soon saw, was different from other men then living. Sometimes they imagined he might indeed be one of the giants of the early centuries returned to the earth again, and at other times they could offer no explanation for his genius, simply exclaiming, "What manner of man is this!" It was because Jesus was different from all other men of his day and generation that he created a sensation which left the nation quivering. If he had repeated the old teachings in the old fashion, he would not have infuriated the Scribes and Pharisees, and brought about the tragedy of Golgotha. He was too original to be endurable, he advanced too many strange and revolutionary ideas to make it safe for the land to hold him; it was because he made all things new that they nailed him to the cross.

Strange to say, the world has come at last to question the originality of Jesus. This is one of the fiercely debated questions of our day. Numerous schools of Bible students have vigorously denied his originality, and with industry and ingenuity have demonstrated that everything he said had been said before, and that to the world of thought he has not contributed a single fresh idea. His language, even, so these men assert, is taken from the poets and the prophets, while every one of his conceptions can be found in the literature of earlier days. To make out their case these deniers of Jesus' originality have ransacked the Old Testament in search of phrases similar to those which Jesus used, and through all the extant writings of the ancient Rabbis they have made their way looking with keen and eager eyes for evidence that Jesus' best ideas were borrowed. Nor has the attention been confined to Hebrew literature alone. The sacred books of distant Oriental lands have been summoned to give their testimony to prove that this Hebrew prophet was after all a plagiarist or an echo. The supposition has been advanced that possibly at some time in his life Jesus may have traveled into India gathering up ideas there for the instruction of his people. According, therefore, to certain writers, Jesus' discourses are a patchwork of quotations. He was a repeater of the wisdom taught by men before his day, an imitator of illustrious orators and poets, a shrewd and talented eclectic who gathered together the gems of many minds and times and dazzled the world by the treasures which he had borrowed.

What shall we say to all this? Was Jesus really original? This subject of originality is always provocative of discussion. No man has ever claimed to be original whose claim has not been disputed. No genius has ever been placed among the thinkers of the world without stirring up a host of critics who have vehemently denied his right to a place there. Molibre is probably the most creative and inventive genius which France has yet produced, but there were Frenchmen in his day, and there have been Frenchmen since his day, who have declared that he stole half his works from the old bookstalls. England's most original poet is Shakespeare, but by his contemporaries he was accused of masquerading in the brilliant plumage of other birds, and there are those who, familiar with the French and Italian writings from which the English poet drew his material, are unwilling to concede the claim that his mind was indeed original. No American writer has been more suggestive than Ralph Waldo Emerson, but to many students of literature he is little more than a gleaner in the wide fields of thought, his essays being counted strings of gems borrowed from the kings and queens of other lands and times. Was Jesus then original? It depends on what you mean by originality. If to be original one must coin words never heard before and speak in phrases which no other tongue has ever used, then

Jesus was not original. He coined no new words and many of his phrases have the flavor of the olden times. Nor was he the proclaimer of ideas that had never entered man's mind before. All his main ideas of God and the soul, of duty, and of destiny had been if not expanded in the writings of the Hebrew poets and prophets at least suggested there, and the principles of conduct which Jesus taught were for the most part the very principles which had been proclaimed by men of God before his day. This may be surprising to those who have not given the subject careful thought, but on reflection you will see that this is just what might reasonably have been expected. If there is a God who loves our race, it is incredible that no correct idea of Deity or the soul, of duty or of destiny, should have entered the human mind before Jesus was born in Bethlehem. Sad indeed it would have been had Jesus, on coming to the earth, found no conceptions in men's minds which corresponded to the truth, and no feelings in their hearts which God could take delight in. The fact is that God has never left himself without a witness. The Son of God has always been in the world. He is the light that lights every man who is born. From the beginning he has been giving men right ideas and right feelings and helping them to reach right conclusions and decisions. We ought, therefore, to expect nothing in Jesus' teaching absolutely unthought of before his incarnation. We ought to expect to find just what we do find, that everything he taught had been anticipated, and that all his cardinal ideas had existed in germ in the writings of holy men who at divers times had been moved by the Holy Spirit. Jesus instead of suggesting ideas never before heard of, and expounding truths of which no man had ever conceived, picked up the ancient writings, declaring that they contain the word of the Almighty and that he had come to interpret their meaning and to fulfil what the poets and prophets had dreamed. He did not come to destroy the old ideas or the old truths. He came to fill full. There had been foreshadowings and anticipations and approximations, and now in the fulness of time God is going to speak His full-toned message through His Son.

It is at this point, then, that we are to look for the originality of Jesus. We shall not find it in his phrases or even in his conceptions, but rather in his emphasis and his manner of reading life and the world. He began by reading an old chapter in Isaiah, but he gave it an emphasis which it had never known before, the result being that it burst upon the congregation in Nazareth with the force of a fresh revelation. Men were reading the Scriptures, but they did not know which words to emphasize. Jesus understood. The result was that the Scripture became new. Religion is partly ceremony and partly ethics. Like all things else on earth, it must have a body and also a spirit. But the leaders of the Jewish church had forgotten the point of emphasis. Jesus knew. By emphasizing mercy instead of sacrifice he made religion new. Men had forgotten how to read the world. There were institutions and there were human beings, and the wisest men of Israel had forgotten which is most important, — an institution or a man. Jesus threw the emphasis on the individual soul and by so doing opened a new epoch in the history of the world.

There was also an accent in his teaching which men had never heard before, not even in the voice of Moses or Elijah. It was the accent of assurance, certainty, authority. It is not the words which a man speaks, but the way in which he speaks them which determines their effect upon the life of the world. No such an accent as that of Jesus had ever before been heard in Palestine. There was never a quaver in his voice. In no discourse was there anything problematic. He never hesitated, speculated, made use of intonations which indicate a wavering mind. He was always positive, certain, infallible. "Verily, verily, I say unto you." Such was the manner of his speech, and it was a manner which he caught from none other.

The new accent and the new emphasis were the product of a new personality. No personality like that of Jesus had ever been encased in flesh before. He was a new man. Even Roman soldiers could feel that he was different from every other man they had ever known. He had all the faculties and passions of our common humanity, and yet no one had ever had them in the combination and in the strength in which they were found in him. Some one has said that in all schools of art an artist is praised not for what is different in him from others, but only for doing most strongly what all are endeavoring. Jesus was man completed. What a fulness of life there was in him! What a power he had. The world. of nature responded to the gentlest touch of his finger-tips. He was different from all other men that had ever been, and he said so. He lifted himself into a unique position and claimed for himself privileges and rights which he denied to all others. He claimed to be the light of the world, the bread of life, the water of life, the only good shepherd, the way, the truth, the life, the only mediator between God and man, the only one who knows deity completely and who can save the world from its sins. Here we strike something which is unique and in every sense original. No other man had ever spoken after this fashion either in Palestine or out of it. No language like this was ever heard in India or anywhere else. There is nothing even resembling this in the greatest of the Hebrew poets or prophets. It is when Jesus speaks of himself that we catch a note original in the music of our world. When you hear some one challenging the originality of Jesus and talking about the parallel passages to be found in the rabbinical writers, ask for a few parallel passages corresponding to the paragraphs in the Gospels in which Jesus declares what he is.

John, who knew him best, heard him saying, "Behold I make all things new." He could say this because he was new himself. Not having our infirmities and fears, our frailties and our sins, his eyes see things as ours do not see them, and his heart has feelings which we but dimly understand. He says, "Come unto me and I will make all things new!" He does it by giving us a changed attitude to life, by teaching us how to shift the emphasis from words unimportant to words important, and by showing us the insignificance of show and form compared with the qualities of a loving heart, by taking away our fears which stand round us like grim Kings of Night, and substituting in their places the angels of Faith and Hope, by striking off our fetters and bringing us into the light and liberty which belong to the sons of God. It is an original work, and only he can do it. He did it for Paul. Paul was a scholar and was familiar with those wonderful rabbinical writings in which certain modern scholars find such stores of treasures. But for some reason these wonderful writings even when taught by the greatest of rabbis did not reach the core of Paul's need, and he kept on crying, "O wretched man that I am, who shall deliver me from the body of this death?" And then one day he met Jesus, and behold, all things became new. From that day to the day of his death Paul urged men to put off the old man and to put on the new man, which after God is created in righteousness and true holiness.

It may be that for some of you life has grown irksome and the world drab and commonplace. Life has lost its sparkle and its zest and the world is no longer to you what Charles Lamb said it was to him, "a very pretty place." The days are threadbare and everything has lost its bloom. What will you do? This is the wise thing to do: Go to Jesus and give yourself afresh to him. Sink your life deeper into his life and catch his ways of seeing things and serving God Take his standpoint, assume his attitude, catch his emphasis, drink in the accent of his voice, and undoubtedly he will do for you what he did for Saul of Tarsus, and what he has done and is doing still for many, — he will make all things new. He unifies human life and simplifies it and elevates it and transforms it and transfigures it, all because he is the Master and the Saviour of the heart. "If any man be in Christ, he is a new creature: old things are passed away: behold all things are become new."

IX: THE NARROWNESS OF JESUS

"Narrow is the way."
— Matthew vii: 14.

Let us think about the narrowness of Jesus. I know it is a disparaging word in our modern speech and damaging to a person's reputation. We often hear it used in a sinister and condemning sense, we sometimes use it so ourselves. We say, "Oh, yes, he is narrow," meaning that one side of his nature has been blighted, blasted. His mind is not full orbed. His heart is not full grown. He is a dwarfed and stunted man, cramped by a defective education or squeezed out of shape by a narrowing environment. In no such sense as this was the man of Galilee narrow. But what word will better express one of the conspicuous traits of Jesus than just this word "narrowness"? He set definite boundaries for himself, he shut himself up within contracted limits; in this sense he was narrow.

How narrow was the circle inside of which he did all his work! He lived his life in Palestine, a little country no larger than Connecticut. It was not a prominent country either, but only a little province tributary to mighty Rome. It cut no figure in the eye of the world, and the lords and ladies of the world's capitals knew little of it and cared less. It was an obscure and rural country, small in territory and insignificant in prestige, and yet the Prince of Glory confined himself to this little corner of the earth. He might have traveled across the world as many an illustrious teacher had done before his day. He might have taught in Athens and lifted up his voice in the streets of the Eternal City. He might have given his message to a wide circle of men whose influence covered many lands; but he rather chose to stay at home, to give his time to the cities of Galilee, to pour out his strength on the villages of Judea. For thirty years he remained in the dingy obscurity of a carpenter's shop, and the country upon which he poured out the full wealth of his brain and heart was only a carpenter's shop among the palaces of the earth.

If his field was contracted, so also was the character of his work. He only tried to do one thing. There were a thousand good things which a good man in Palestine might have done, but he left nine hundred and ninety-nine of them unattempted and confined himself to the one thing which he believed his Heavenly Father had given him to do. Men did not understand such narrowness. They were always urging him to swing into a wider orbit and do something which would create a greater stir. A man one day interrupted him while he was speaking, saying, "Make my brother divide the inheritance with me!" But his reply was, "That lies outside my province — come and listen to me and I will do for you the service which God has appointed me to do." It was a noble piece of work which this interrupter asked the prophet of Nazareth to perform. An injustice had been perpetrated, and what is nobler in this world than the redressing of a wrong? Wrongs ought to be righted and injustices ought to give way to justice. It was a righteous piece of work which the man wanted to have done, but it was not Christ's work, and therefore he would not do it. No one man can do everything, no one man should attempt everything. There are a thousand things which need to be done and yet which no man however industrious and noble can perform. Jesus set limits to his activity, and beyond those limits no man ever persuaded him to go. One day his brothers wanted him to go to Jerusalem and make an impression on the big men there, but he refused to listen to their exhortation, telling them that they might go any time they chose, but that it was different with him. He could not go until it was time for him to go, until his work compelled him to go. He could not go until his hour had come. When the hour arrived he set his face steadfastly to go to Jerusalem. All along the way men tried to divert him, but he could not be diverted, to Jerusalem he must go. He had a baptism to be baptized with and he was pressed in on both sides and there was no relief until his work had been accomplished. He always speaks like a man whose feet are on a narrow path. Men all around him have the enjoyment of large liberty. They wander hither and thither, going whithersoever they wish, but it was not so with him. He could not dissipate his energy, he could not waste a single hour. It was always, "I must," "I must," "I must." There were broad roads on his right and left, and along these roads thousands of his countrymen were travelling, but he could not go with them. It was for him to walk along the narrow path, for this alone led to the glorious life which was to cheer and save the world. When he talks to men about the two ways, one of them narrow and the other one broad, he is speaking out of his own experience; and when he urges men to choose the narrow one in preference to the one which is broad, he is only saying, "Follow me!"

In the realm of the intellect he chose the way which was narrow. There is a feeling now prevalent that it is unwise for a man to confine himself to any one religion or any one particular statement of belief. It is better — so men say — not to pin your faith to the sleeve of any one idea or truth, but hold yourself in readiness to accept every idea which may come your way. Keep the windows and doors of your mind wide open and let everything blow through which the winds may be able to catch up, but do not settle down upon any definite conceptions of God or the soul, of duty or destiny, because in so doing you narrow yourself and may ultimately degenerate into a bigot. With this sort of philosophy Jesus of Nazareth had no sympathy. To him certain conceptions of God were true and others were false, certain estimates of man were correct and others erroneous, certain standards of duty were uplifting and others degrading, and with all his mind and soul and strength he clung to the true and combated the false. He never shrank from holding clean-cut opinions and from expressing them with vigor and emphasis. He was not afraid of being called intolerant or a bigot. He made a distinction between falsehood and truth, and was not ashamed to stamp upon the former and proclaim boldly the latter. Errors he struck no matter who held them, and hallucinations he repudiated no matter by how many accepted. In many a modern circle he would have been counted a narrow man, for he made no compromises, and he would not bend, and he maintained with unflinching persistency the things which his heart knew to be true and good. If to be dogmatic is to be positive, then he was the most dogmatic teacher who ever brought men to his feet. He swept other leaders and teachers out of the way with gorgeous sweeps of scorn. "Other men," he said, "have taught you this and that, but I say unto you." And when his hearers, amazed by the boldness of his speech, lifted their eyes, they saw that he had placed himself above even Moses and the prophets. He would not allow his followers to roam at their will through the realms of thought, accepting everything or nothing at their own whim or fancy; but he taught them day after day certain definite, and positive conceptions and principles to which they must cling or else lose their souls. He came to bear witness to the truth, and for that reason he was not broad enough to give a place in his heart to falsehood.

This same narrowness comes out again in the limited range of his approbations. There were some things he could praise and there were other things he was obliged to condemn. There were some men he could eulogize, and there were other men fit for nothing but burning condemnation. He did not wear a universal smile. He did not group men together as though they were all alike. He made distinctions, and he taught other men to make them too. There is a weak and sentimental way of lumping men together and trying to make it appear that men are all substantially alike and that one is not so much better after all than another. Jesus' estimate was the product of severe discrimination. He had eyes which saw through the exterior of men's hearts, and he judged them with a fearlessness which made them crouch in terror. The gang of thieves who carried on their business in the temple were driven out in bewilderment and consternation. To some of the most influential men of Jerusalem he said, "You are fools and blind men, you are serpents, you are vipers!" Between some men and other men there was a great gulf fixed. He did not minimize the heinousness of sin by treating all men alike. It makes no difference to some of us whether men are honest or not, or whether they live filthy lives or not; but it made a difference to Jesus. No mean and contemptible scoundrel ever felt in Jesus' presence like holding up his head. He was so narrow in his judgments he refused to let bad men feel that they were good. In all his judgments on the lives and homes of men he pursued the narrow way.

It is in his habit of drawing distinctions and setting boundaries that we are to find the cause of many things which might otherwise remain inexplicable. One of the notes of Jesus' life was joy. He was a man acquainted with grief, and yet his joy was without measure. It was one of the things he had so much of that he could bequeath it to his disciples. Could he have been happy had he not walked within narrow limits? What period in any man's life is so wretched as that which lies in the later teens or early twenties in which he does not know what he is going to do? The big wide world lies stretched out before him with uncounted possibilities, and the young man full of vigor and ambition, capable of doing a hundred different things, is wretched. There are a hundred doors which he can open, but he does not know which one to try. There are a hundred fields in which he can expend his strength, but he cannot decide which field to enter. There are a hundred enterprises he feels sure he could lead to victory, but he cannot decide which one is most worthy of his leadership. And of all mortals such a youth is most miserable. No man can be happy with an entire world to roam over. It is only when a man picks out some particular little sphere and says, "Inside of this I purpose to work," that real life begins and his heart learns the art of singing. So long as the world's work lies in a mountain mass, there is only depression and hopelessness; it is when a man picks up in his hand a definite, tiny task and says, "This is the thing to which I shall devote my life," that the shadows vanish and life becomes worth living. It is the narrow path that leads to life. Jesus' work was definite. At twelve he knew the business to which he must give himself. There never was a day on which he allowed himself to be inveigled into doing something else. Right here is where we are prone to blunder, and it is at this point that we should look for the root cause of much of the disquiet in our souls. We start out to do a certain work and immediately people begin to say: "Why don't you do this?" "Come and do this!" and before we are aware of our folly we have dissipated our energy in trying to do things which God never intended us to attempt. It is here that we blunder in our benevolences. We try to give to many causes, and the result is we have little joy as the result of our giving. It is no man's duty to contribute to every good cause that passes his way, and it is only when we draw a circle around our beneficence that we become what God likes to see — a cheerful giver. If you want to see a man who sings at his work, look for him inside of a narrow circle.

Not only was Jesus joyful, but he was mighty. He made an impression because he stayed in one place, and hit the same nail on the head until it was driven completely in. Had he wandered over the earth speaking his parables, they would have fallen into more ears but would have moulded fewer hearts. By staying in Palestine and keeping his heart close to a few chosen hearts, he became increasingly influential so that the authorities were frightened, fearing that he might overturn the nation. The men who were the nearest to him became so passionately in love with him that they were ready to die for him. He made himself thus mighty by limiting himself. It is with men as it is with rivers: a river becomes a river only by the assistance of its banks. The difference between a river and a swamp is that a river has banks and a swamp has none. Take away its banks and the river becomes a swamp. Many a river becomes mightier and more majestic because the mountains press in upon it. Left to sprawl out over the plains it had become shallow, muddy, feeble; but when the mountains pressed in upon it, narrowing its channel and crowding the waters in upon themselves, the river took on a new depth and strength of current, girding itself as it were to turn the wheels of mighty mills and to carry the ships of commerce to the sea. "Thou hast enlarged me when I was in distress," the Hebrew poet cries, and many a man can say the same. It is when our life by some sorrow or calamity or fresh responsibilities is compressed within a narrower channel that it takes on interior richness and gains a significance which it never had before.

By limiting himself our Lord came off conqueror. He succeeded. What is it to succeed? It is to do the thing for which we were created. The most galling of all experiences is the failure to do that which is most worth while. Jesus attempted to do one thing only, and that was to perform the work which his Father had given him to do. At the end of his life he could look into his Father's face and say, "I have finished the work which thou gavest me to do." It was indeed time that the Father should glorify the Son! Jesus' life on earth covered only thirty-three brief years, and yet he did the greatest piece of work ever accomplished on the earth. It is wonderful what a stupendous task can be accomplished in a little time if a man is only willing to keep at it. We mourn unwisely when we mourn disconsolately over lives that seem to be cut off at noon. Let a man strive not to live long but to do his work, and if he does it why should we lament because he dies at noon?

We have been touching upon a great principle, — the principle which lies at the basis of all the fine arts. The arts which are called fine become fine because of the narrowness of the limitations which they impose. They all subject the soul to a discipline which is severe, and insist upon a bondage which cannot be broken through. In music there is no leeway left to the singer. He cannot sing a little sharp or a little flat and still produce music. In music everything is precise, exact, severe, and all the tones must take accurately the precise points assigned them by the master, else the music does not have in it that indescribable power which lifts and entrances the soul. The artist cannot dip his brush as he pleases into this color or that, careless as to how much of this or how little of that he spreads on the canvas. He is held in the grip of laws which he cannot violate even a little without marring the picture. It is the narrow way on which artists must forever walk. Why is it so much more difficult to write poetry than prose? It is because poetry subjects the soul to a severer bondage. The poet must submit to a discipline of which the prose writer knows nothing. The rules of accent and rhythm and melody are inexorable and only genius has strength enough to obey them all. Poets must walk the narrow path. But the most difficult of all the fine arts is the high art of living as God would have a mortal to live. Singing is easy and so is painting compared with this exacting, soul-taxing art of living. One cannot think anything he pleases, or feel as he wants to, or act as he is inclined to. He must walk the narrow path. Jesus walked it, and he calls men everywhere to become his followers. He is rigorous in his demands. He is inexorable in his commands. He is despotic in the limitations which he imposes. He says, "Come unto me!" We ask, cannot we go to others? His reply is, There are no others. Come to me! And when we come he says, "Follow me!" We hesitate and ask, "Is this really necessary, can we not choose an easier way?" His reply is: "Follow me." "If you do not take up your cross and follow me, you cannot be my disciple, and no one comes to the Father except through me." He says, "Abide in me!" and we demur and wonder if after all it is necessary to shut ourselves up in what seems to be so narrow and limited a sphere. But he says to us with that strange, dogmatic, compelling accent which stirred the hearts of the people long ago in Galilee, "Verily I say unto you, unless you abide in me, you have no life at all in you!" This, then, is the narrowness of Jesus. He is narrow for a purpose. He limited himself, emptied himself of his divine glory, was found in the fashion of a man, walked the narrow path which led from the carpenter's shop to Golgotha, all because of his great love for us, and in order that we might each one of us have life and have it more abundantly.

X: THE BREADTH OF JESUS

"Preach the Gospel to the whole creation,"
— Mark xvi: 15.

There is a sense in which Jesus of Nazareth was lacking in breadth. He had apparently no desire to see the world, and was content to spend his life in little Palestine. He walked a path which was narrow, and refused to give his approbation to men and measures which won the esteem and praise of thousands of his countrymen. But there was a purpose in this narrowness, and a reason for it. His narrowness was a product of his breadth. He walked the narrow path because he carried in his heart the dream of an empire which was vast. By standing in one place and striking repeatedly the strings of the same set of hearts, he started vibrations which have filled the world with music. By carefully tending the fire which he had kindled, he made it hot enough to change the spiritual climate of many lands. By saturating a little circle of chosen followers with his spirit, he made them capable of carrying on their shoulders a lost race to God. By persistently treading a single path, he made that path so luminous that every eye can see it; by discarding false ideas and by opposing wicked men, he has made it easier for truth seekers and the soldiers of God in each succeeding generation to fight a good fight and to win the crown. By being faithful in a few things, he won the place of Lordship over many cities; and by limiting himself, and by making himself of no reputation, he founded a kingdom broad as humanity and of which there shall be no end. If you study the New Testament, you will see that this man from the beginning carried the world in his eye and the race on his heart. What strange paradoxes one finds in the realm of the soul. If you would be broad, then be narrow. Jesus was narrow because his breadth was immeasurable.

It was the breadth of Jesus' ideas and sympathies which first brought him into conflict with his countrymen. The Jews as a people were proverbially narrow and bigoted. They divided the world into two parts and placed an almost impassable gulf between themselves and all other races. Inside of Palestine people were divided into classes by lines which were straight and unchangeable. Hearts were narrow, and feelings were bitter and hard.

Samaria was counted accursed, and men of Galilee on their way to Jerusalem crossed over the Jordan in order that their feet might not be contaminated by treading the Samaritan soil. The Jews were an exclusive and haughty and aristocratic race, constantly thanking God that they were superior to all other nations. But the spirit of Jesus was different. In his very first sermon in Nazareth he called attention to the fact that in the days of Elijah, God had picked out a widow outside the promised land for special consideration and honor, and that in the days of Elisha, although there were many lepers in Israel, God had passed by them all, and healed a Gentile leper, Naaman, the Syrian. It was all written down in their Scriptures, but the good people in Nazareth, like many other good people since their day, did not pay attention to many things written in their own Scriptures, and when Jesus began to eulogize the widow of Sidon and the Syrian king, their hearts became so hot within them that they broke up the meeting and tried to mob the preacher. They hustled him down through the narrow street and out along a road which ran near the brink of a precipice, fully intending to crowd him over the edge, but he foiled their nefarious intentions and made his escape to Capernaum. This is really the beginning of Jesus' conflict with the world. It is worth while to remember that the first antagonism was occasioned by his effort to push out men's horizon. The narrow-headed villagers of Nazareth were driven to the edge of murder by the breadth of a mind which went beyond them.

The amplitude of Jesus' ideas is evidenced by their perennial freshness and applicability to all kinds of men and conditions. How wonderful it is that Jesus' ideas are broad enough to cover all the nations and all the centuries. Many ideas shrivel and dry up with the lapse of time. Political ideas have a strange fashion of passing away, and so do scientific ideas. One century has no interest in the political teachings of the century which preceded it, and no generation is willing to accept the science of the generation that went before it. But the ideas of Jesus have such breadth that they can cover the world and the ages, and although nineteen centuries have swept away almost everything which was believed and taught in Jesus' day, his ideas are still alive and the very words in which they are expressed seem destined to outlive the stars. This is indeed strange, that we people of the twentieth century should be a part of the Nazareth congregation, listening to the very ideas which interested Jews nearly two thousand years ago, and so broad are these ideas and so universally applicable to the demands of the mind and the needs of the heart that each succeeding generation down to the end of time will take its place in the congregation of the prophet of Nazareth, so that if one could see the whole history unrolled before him, he would discover the countless millions of humanity gathered round a single teacher, and that teacher none other than the teacher whom the people of Nazareth tried to kill. Broad, indeed, must be the ideas which can cover all peoples and kindreds and tongues throughout all the eras of their existence.

And his heart was as far-reaching as his brain. The social sympathies of Jesus were to his countrymen a surprise and a scandal. He felt with everybody. He seemed to be ignorant of the proprieties and the etiquette of well-bred people. His heart went out to all sorts and conditions of men in a way which was reckless and shocking. There were men in Palestine who were under the ban of public opinion. Every right-thinking man despised them. They were treated like the dogs in the street. They had feelings, but nobody felt with them. Every door of society was slammed in their face. These men were known as Publicans. Jesus' heart went out to these men. He talked with them, ate with them. Not content with this he took one of them into the inner circle of his intimate friends and allowed him to go out and teach and work in his name. Even in Jericho, the narrowest of all Judean cities, because for centuries it had been the home of the priests, this big-hearted prophet took dinner with one of the most notorious of all the Publicans, to the consternation of the best people in the land. And not content with thus showing the breadth of his sympathies by his deeds, he painted a picture which hangs in the great art gallery of the world. Its colors will never fade, and no thief can ever destroy it. It is the picture entitled, "The Pharisee and the Publican." The lesson of the picture is that God's heart is more responsive to a penitent Publican than to a vain-glorious Pharisee. There was only one set of men lower than the Publicans, and they were the Samaritans. Every man's hand was against them. Every heart was hard as flint toward them. And Jesus befriended them. He felt with them. He gave religious instruction even to a Samaritan woman, and healed even a Samaritan leper. So wide was his heart that there was room in it for a Samaritan outcast whose flesh was rotten. And as if determined that all the world down to the end of time should know the width of his sympathies, he painted a picture which men will look at as long as they have eyes to see and hearts to feel, and the name of the picture is, "The Good Samaritan." What havoc this man made with the traditions and customs of his countrymen! The land was crossed in all directions by dividing walls and estranging barriers, constructed by narrow-hearted teachers, and after Jesus had walked through the land, lo, the barriers and walls were a mass of ruins. His great, loving heart burst asunder all the regulations and restrictions. There was room in his soul for everybody.

It is in the width of his love that men have found most to wonder at. His love was unbounded. It was an ocean without a shore. He was not willing that his followers should set boundaries to their love, because all such barriers were contrary to his habit and foreign to his spirit. When Peter asked him how often a man ought to forgive another who has trespassed against him, and suggested seven as a number almost grotesquely large, being more than (twice the number suggested by the most liberal of the rabbis, Jesus said: "Do not set any limits at all. There are no boundaries in the realm of love. You cannot calculate in the empire of the heart. Mathematics is foreign to affection." Whenever he spoke about love he said something which amazed his hearers. One day he said, "Love your enemies; bless them that curse you; do good to them that hate you; and pray for them that despitefully use you and persecute you." And when men stood aghast showing by their faces that only God could be expected to have a love so broad, Jesus went on to add that God is to be the model of all men who want to live right, and that one's constant aim shall be to bring his life up to God's style, and to imitate Him in the unbounded reach of His good will. Nor was this simply exhortation. It was not only preaching but practice. Jesus taught forgiveness because he knew the blessedness of a forgiving heart. He himself was forgiving always. He had no grudges, no retaliations, no revenges. Some men forgive because they have not eyes to see the heinousness of wrong, and not heart to feel its devilishness. Jesus saw the loathsomeness of vice, knew the odiousness of vulgarity, felt the hideousness of sin. His heart was so sensitive that it blazed against evil, but while he loathed the sin he could love the sinner, and so when his executioners nailed his hands and feet to the cross, the only word which escaped his lips was, "Forgive," "Forgive," "Forgive." That great word contained the blood of his heart.

It is this abounding love which accounts for the immeasurable reaches of his hope. He was the most hopeful of all teachers. No matter how dull the pupil, he still believed that he would learn. Men had grown cynical and pessimistic in Palestine nineteen centuries ago. They had lost confidence in humanity, and had settled down in the conviction that for many mortals we can expect nothing but perdition. To the religious teachers of Palestine certain classes were beyond redemption. They were lost and were labeled "Lost." It was known throughout the city that to certain sinners no exhortation could be directed, no promise could be offered. The Jewish church turned its back upon all such, and confined itself to men who could be saved. But Jesus, because he loved, also hoped. His hope was as immeasurable as his love. He did not reject the refuse of society. He saw promise even in the scum. The dregs of society are not to be carelessly tossed away. There is a chance for the man who is supposed to have no chance, there is hope for the man whom men have doomed to perdition. You cannot tell what is in a man by what he says or even by what he does. There is more in him than comes out in his words and his deeds. And so Jesus proceeded to show that the so-called lost men were not lost, and that even in blasted Samaria the fields were white to the harvest. He did not hesitate to direct his most earnest exhortations to men who were supposed to have no heart, and even when the world's cruelty was cutting into him like steel, he said, "I, if I be lifted up, will draw all men unto me." So boundless was his confidence in man, that he set no limits to his expectations.

He could not accomplish the redemption of the world in the few years of his earthly career, but he would form a society, baptize it with his spirit, and through this society God from His throne in heaven would redeem the race. The formation of this Christian society is one of the great events of the New Testament. The character of the men built into it has a wealth of suggestion. If you were going to form an organization for the purpose of carrying out your ideas after your death, what kind of men would you select? You would — I suspect — choose men like yourself, of your own social circle, and of your own type of mind, and of your own general temperament and make-up, and in so doing you would have a society which would come to nothing. Mark the method of Jesus. He chooses men of all grades and from all classes. No man in the group is like any of his comrades, and no one of them is like Jesus. There is a mercurial man, Peter; and there is a lymphatic man, Thomas. There is a fire-eater, Simon Zelotes, a member of the fieriest political party in Palestine; and there is the prosaic and slow-going Philip. There is a man of good family and spotless reputation, John; and by his side is a man with a tarnished name, Matthew, the Publican. All temperaments are here, and all combinations of mental faculties, and here are representatives from various classes and divers social strata. In doing a wide work you must have a broad instrument, and the Christian church as it left the hands of Jesus embraced in its membership the types of men which would be able to open all the doors. Never does the breadth of the mind of Jesus come out with more startling clearness than in the manner of his choices in the formation of the society which was to bear his name and carry on his work. It was a great work, the vastest which has ever entered into the heart of man. He had constantly the ends of the earth in his eye. The narrowness of the petty men who administered the affairs of the Jewish church distressed him. "Many," he said, "shall come from the East and the West and from the North and the South and shall sit down with Abraham and Isaac and Jacob in the Kingdom of God." At an early stage he told his apostles not to go outside the limits of their own people in their work, but this limitation of field was only educational, and with their increasing strength was to pass forever away. Men should stay in Jerusalem long enough to secure strength sufficient to grapple with the problems of Judea, and they should tarry in Judea until they were capable of grappling with the more difficult conditions of Samaria, and they should work in Samaria until they had acquired the endurance which would enable them to travel to the uttermost parts of the earth. In the earlier stages a teacher does not communicate to the pupil his plans for the years which lie far ahead. Jesus did not talk to his apostles about the world and the ages on the day of their baptism or even in the upper chamber, but before he left the earth he poured into their ear the great message which had been in his heart from the beginning, and it ran thus, "Go preach the Gospel to the whole creation." All national boundaries are now obliterated and the horizon thrown round the apostles is not less narrow than the large circle of the world. "Go disciple the nations." It was in this manner that he spoke to them before the cloud received him from their sight, and whenever from that day to this the followers of Jesus have been closest to him, they have been found to be dreaming of conquests wide as the world.

He that hath seen this man hath seen the Father. In Jesus of Nazareth we get a revelation of the breadth of the heart of the Eternal. How did it happen that Jesus was so spacious in his ideas and so broad in his sympathies and so far-reaching in his plannings? It was because God was in him revealing Himself to men. That is what God always is — broad in His sympathies, wonderful in His expectations, boundless in His love. He so loved the world that He gave His only begotten Son — and this Son came to earth and tasted death for every man — and the Spirit whom He sent and also the bride who is His church, they keep on crying through the centuries: "Come! Let him that is athirst come. Whosoever will, let him take the water of life freely."

This, then, is a message for us all. No matter who you are, you have a sure place in the mind and heart of God. No matter how you have sinned, you are inside the boundaries of His sympathy. No matter what you have said or felt or thought or done, you are still the object of His love. No matter how often you have disappointed Him, He is still expecting of you better things. Whoever you are, and wherever you are, and whatever you are, you are included in His plans. When He laid down the lines of His vast scheme for humanity, you were not overlooked or forgotten. When He framed His church, a place inside of it was assigned to you. That place will remain vacant until you fill it. You cannot escape Him. His arms are all-embracing. The width of His heart is infinite. His love is everlasting,

"I know not where his islands lift
Their fronded palms in air;
I only know I cannot drift
Beyond his love and care."

XI: JESUS' TRUST IN GOD

"He trusted on God."
— Matthew xxvii: 43.

We are trying to see Jesus as he was. It is surprising that we do not know him better when his image is so vividly portrayed for us in the Gospels. The very familiarity of the story has a deadening effect upon the mind. We have heard so much of Jesus ever since the days of childhood, have heard so many teachers and preachers speak about him, that the mind has hardened and refuses to be impressed by him. Many of us have had faulty methods of Bible study. We have studied the Bible piecemeal, in scraps and patches, getting a knowledge of isolated passages and never putting together the various parts so as to see Jesus as a man among men. We have caught, it may be, one trait of his lovely character; we have fixed our gaze upon one bright particular star, and have missed the sweep and swing of the constellations; we have picked up a pebble now and then and have failed to take in the curve of the vast shore and the swell and surge of the sea. Our object in all these studies is to see him as he was seen by the men of his time.

We have already found in him the note of strength and the note of gladness, and now let us get a little deeper and find out if we can the spring from which strength and gladness flow. How does it happen that this man was so masterful in every situation, and how did it come to pass that he was joyful in the midst of so many shadows? The answer to the question lies written broad on all the pages of the New Testament. His strength and gladness came from his steadfast trust in God. If you were to ask me what is deepest and most fundamental in the character of Jesus, I should say, it was his trust in God. I see not how any one can read the New Testament without feeling that this to him was the Alpha and the Omega, the first and the last. It was the heaven above his head, the earth beneath his feet, the atmosphere he daily breathed, the spirit in which he was saturated, the music that ran through all his conversation, the inspiration of all his life. Possibly no better testimony upon this point can be found in all the Scriptures than that taken from the lips of his deadliest foes. We have already found these enemies of Jesus valuable witnesses, and they will not disappoint us here. When he was dying on the cross many people laughed at him and wagged their heads, saying derisive and spiteful things. Among these people, strange to say, there were members of the Sanhedrim, chief priests, scribes and leaders — they all ridiculed and scorned him, and the climax of their vituperation was this, "He trusted on God!" No blacker jeer ever was belched forth from the jaws of hell than that. It is incredible that human beings could be so diabolical as to sneer at a man in the hour of death; but that is what the religious leaders of Palestine did when the Prophet of Galilee was dying. The dark and terrible sentence throws a blaze of light upon the teaching and the conduct of Jesus. His whole course of action had made upon the people among whom he moved the impression that he trusted in God.

Should you ask me for illustrations of this trust, I should be embarrassed not because there are so few but because there are so many. One can dip into the Gospels where he will and find things which bear testimony to Jesus' trust in God. When only a boy he said to his mother, "Wist ye not that I must be about my Father's business?" His last words upon the cross were, "Father, into thy hands I commend my spirit." From that first point to the last point the music of his trust was never broken. He is everywhere and always a man of prayer. At the crises of his life we find him praying. At his baptism and the transfiguration, in the garden, on the cross, he is pouring out his soul to God. Before every important action, in the midst of every difficult situation, at the completion of every stage of work, we find him praying. It was a common thing in Palestine for men to pray, but no man had ever prayed like this man, with such simplicity, with such earnestness, with such boundless trust. Men gathered round him awestruck and said, "Master, teach us how to pray." All Hebrew children were taught to pray from earliest infancy. Prayer was an indispensable feature of Hebrew piety, but men who had prayed from earliest youth felt when they heard this man pray that they had never prayed at all. The word which he applied to God was Father. Only occasionally in the long sweep of the ages had a soul here and there ventured to apply to Deity a name so familiar and sweet, but Jesus of Nazareth always thinks and speaks of God as Father. He names Him this in his own prayers, he tells other men that they also may use this name. To trust in the goodness and mercy of the good Father was his own intensest and fullest delight; to induce others to trust in Him also was his constant ambition and endeavor.

How much Jesus has to teach us at this point. It is often supposed that it is easy to believe in God. The fact is, nothing is more difficult to do at certain times and in certain circumstances. It is easy, indeed, to say that one trusts in God, but really to do it when justice seems dead and love seems to have vanished, that is difficult indeed. Who can study Nature without finding things in it which make it difficult to believe in the good Father? Does not Nature seem to be cruel? Does she seem to have any heart? Do not fire burn and water drown and volcanoes cover cities without mercy? Does Nature not carry on her vast operations with absolute indifference to the wishes or welfare of men? All of the great thinkers who have gazed into the face of Nature have been appalled by her heartlessness and her indifference. Jesus of Nazareth found in Nature fresh evidences of God's love. Other men noting how the sunshine falls upon the heads of the good and the bad had come to the conclusion that God does not know — God does not care. Whereas Jesus looking on the same phenomenon sees in it fresh evidence of the great heart of the good Father. The rain falls upon the farm of the man who blasphemes and also upon the farm of the man who serves God, not because God is indifferent to the difference in character, but because he is so good that his mercy covers all of his children. Just as the earthly parent allows the disobedient son to sit down at the table with his obedient brothers and sisters, so it is the good God who feeds the good and the bad, the just and the unjust, unwilling to show resentment, hoping still that every heart will surrender. To Jesus Nature is a great witness, clothed in light, bearing continuous testimony to the width of the eternal mercy.

But if Nature seems indifferent and cruel, what shall we say of history — the arena in which has been played out the tragedy of human life? What a jumble of mysteries! What a mass of woes! All of the centuries groaning with agony, all of the ages dripping with blood! Who can look upon the sufferings of the innocent, or hear the cries of the oppressed, or witness the slaughter of the pure and the good without asking himself: Does God know? Does God care? Right forever on the scaffold, wrong forever on the throne, — so it seems to the man who reads history. Vice triumphs over virtue, dishonesty tramples upon honesty, injustice lords it over justice, hate defies and defeats love. This happens not once but ten thousand times. Some men read the dark and terrible story and give up their faith in God. Jesus looks upon the same scene and gives to it a different interpretation. He sees good men come and offer their services to the world only to be rejected and repulsed. One of them is stoned, another is beaten, another is killed. Their dead bodies are piled up in sickening heaps, but to Jesus this is not evidence of the indifference of God — it is the proof of his long-suffering patience; it is because he is not willing that any should be lost that he keeps on century after century, sending into the world prophets and apostles, heroes and saints, who shall proclaim the message of heaven to bewildered and sinful man.

But if the processes of Nature and the courses of history make war upon one's trust in God, much more terrible is the conflict which is often necessitated by one's own personal experience. Many a man has for years trusted in God only to discover when evil fortune came that his trust was not strong enough to stand the shock. The very best and strongest of men when overtaken by misfortune are obliged to readjust their faith. For a while they are stupefied and dazed, scarcely knowing whither to turn or what to think. So it was with Job. His faith in God was complete, so he thought; but when his children were taken and his fortune was swept away and his health vanished, he lay upon the ground in his misery crying to God in his pain, unable to see Him either on the right hand or on the left, either behind or before. Many things conspire to blot out one's trust in God. Disappointment may do it, a man's fondest dream may come to nothing, his central ambition may fail. One disappointment after another may come upon him until he sinks down vanquished and hopeless, his torch extinguished. Persecution may break a man's faith in God, the inhumanity of man may turn sour the juices of the heart; the misunderstandings and misrepresentations of men, their hostility and faithlessness, their contempt and their scorn, may render it well-nigh impossible to believe that God rules the world.

Other men are overcome by failure. Nothing to them was so sweet as success. To win success they give the best of their years and all their powers, but in spite of all they can do success does not come. At the end of the day they confess themselves defeated. In the bitterness of their defeat they cry out, "Where is God?" Jesus of Nazareth had all the dark experiences which it is possible for the soul to have. He had a work to do to which he gave all the energy of his brain and his heart. He had a dream which filled him with enthusiasm, he had a message to communicate which he was certain would drive away the gloom and the woe of the world. He went to Jerusalem to announce it — the door there was slammed in his face. He announced it in the synagogues of Galilee, but the people there would not receive it. He then preached it on the street corners of the great cities, but the crowds melted away like snow banks in June. There were at last only twelve men who stood by him, and the hearts of these were so fluctuating that he said, "Will ye also go away?" To these twelve men he gave himself with passionate devotion, pouring into their souls his own very life. But the boldest of them turned out a coward, and one of the most trusted of them became a traitor, and when the crisis in his life came they all forsook him and fled.

But notwithstanding his disappointment, his trust in God was unbroken. In the midst of the tempest his torch kept on burning, and he cried, "Be of good cheer, I have overcome the world." He was persecuted as no other man before his day or since; he was maligned, abused, execrated. Men called him crazy, others said he had a devil. He was accused of blasphemy, of treason — but his heart remained sweet. Men buffeted him and abused him, hissing at him their ingratitude and hatred, but he said, "The cup which my Father has given me to drink, shall I not drink it?" And then finally he failed. He failed to do the thing to which he had devoted all of his powers — the thing for which he had steadfastly prayed. We do not often enough ponder this — that the earthly life of Jesus was a failure. We dwell upon the things which have happened since his death, and dwelling upon these we see that he has succeeded; but it should never be forgotten that his life on the day of his death was a terrible and heart-breaking failure. Injustice was stronger than justice, unrighteousness was mightier than righteousness, hate was stronger than love. He had tried to induce the world to accept a beautiful truth, but the world spurned him. In the hour of his great defeat he still looked to God saying, "Not my will but thine be done." Defeat itself could not daunt him or make him draw back. If it is necessary, he said, that I should be sacrificed, that I should be trodden under the feet of the men who are thirsting for my blood, if that is the will of the Infinite Father, then to that I gladly submit.

Never was there a man like this man. Other great and strong men have lived and labored, but never a man like Jesus of Nazareth. John the Baptist was mighty, but when the wind blew he bent like a reed. Simon Peter was a giant, but when the storm raged he began to sink. But Jesus of Nazareth, in the midst of the wildest storm that ever blotted out the heavens and caused the earth to quake, looked steadily toward God, saying, "Not my will but thine be done." Look down across the ages and see the great men, how they are swayed and tossed by the winds and storms; but there above them all there rises this man of Galilee like some majestic mountain, his peaceful head outlined against the blue.

XII: THE BROTHERLINESS OF JESUS

"First be reconciled to thy brother."
— Matthew v: 24.

We are trying to see Jesus as his contemporaries saw him, and desire to understand if we can the secret of that fascination which he exerted over those that knew him, and to fathom if possible the heart of that magic by which he has thrilled and held nineteen Christian centuries. We have found that the secret of his joy and strength lay in his implicit trust in God, and now I wish to think with you about another trait for which it is difficult for me to find a satisfying name. I should say that it is the love of Jesus were not the word "love" so ambiguous and so liable to misinterpretation; I should say it was the service of Jesus were it not for the fact that service is rather cold and has long since been worn into shreds; I should say the pity of Jesus, but pity is love looking downward, and that does not convey all the truth; I should call it the humanity of Jesus, but that is a vague and indefinite word that does not tell the story vividly; I should say the kindness of Jesus, but the word does not carry with it force enough. Possibly we cannot do better than to take the word "brotherliness," for this word contains two elements, both of which are essential if we would understand the kind of man Jesus was. Brotherliness carries in it not only a sense of kinship but likewise a disposition to render help. There is a relationship and likewise a helpfulness, and both of these blended into one constitute the quality to which I invite your attention now.

That this trait in Jesus made a profound impression upon his contemporaries is evidenced not only by what his friends have said about him, but also by the criticisms and sneers which he drew from his foes. It was a common taunt of the Scribes and Pharisees that he was a friend of Publicans and sinners, and when he hung dying on the cross the leading men of the Jewish church gathered round him saying with a jeer, "He saved others, he cannot save himself." Both of these accusations are as devilish as anything to be found in the literature of the world, but they are valuable to us in this that they show conclusively what impression this man of Galilee made upon the people of his time. It had been his practice all the way through life to help men. He had been a friendly, brotherly man even to the lowest and the basest of society. That was a characteristic which had created a great scandal and made him hateful to many of the respectable people of his day. The same trait is characterized in a famous phrase written by one of his dearest friends, "He went about doing good." What more beautiful eulogy has ever been written about a man than that? With what more lovely wreath of roses could you cover a man's career? In these three sentences — "The friend of Publicans and sinners," "He saved others, he cannot save himself," "He went about doing good" — we get eloquent testimony to the fact that Jesus had a brotherly heart.

Let us look into this accusation, that he was the friend of Publicans and sinners, and find out what it meant. The word "publican" means nothing to us because we have no class of men corresponding to the Publicans of Palestine. They were the tax-gatherers of the country, gathering taxes for the Roman government. They were the hirelings of great capitalists into whose hands it was necessary to turn over a certain sum of money each year, and by extortion and other dishonest measures they could make as much more money for themselves. To every pious Hebrew these men were traitors to their country, and wherever they went they were an object of abhorrence, hatred, and scorn. Their money was tainted money, it would not be accepted in the synagogue. Their oath was absolutely worthless, they could not be a witness in any court of law. If a man promised to do a thing for a Publican under oath, he was not bound to keep his oath. They were set up in the pillory of scorn and execration, and pelted with sneers by every passer-by. They were looked upon as wild beasts in human shape. They were outcasts, vagabonds, worse than the homeless curs that roamed the streets. No decent man would have anything to do with them, no religious teacher took any interest in them. They were simply the offscouring and dregs of society.

But even with these Jesus made friends. Not only did he speak to them but he ate with them, went into their houses and sat down to the table with them — the very climax of audacity! It is one thing to throw money to depraved men as we would throw carrots to bears in a bear pit, it is another thing to eat with them. It is one thing to talk down to bad men, giving them good advice, and quite another thing to associate with them. No one found fault with President Roosevelt so long as he spoke to negroes in the street; it was when he sat down with a negro in the White House that the South blazed with indignation. But this man Jesus sat down and ate with

Publicans, he crossed the chasm over which no man of his day or generation was willing to pass. By doing this he lost his reputation. In the words of an apostle he made himself of no reputation, he took his good name and tore it into shreds and threw it away and all because he was determined to be brotherly. Notwithstanding these men were so base he recognized in them his brothers. They belonged to him and he belonged to them. They were members of the human race, children of the great family of God, and therefore in spite of all that they had done, and notwithstanding all that they were, he treated them as brothers. Not only did this conduct make a profound impression upon the men of Jesus' day, but it has made such a deep impression on all succeeding generations that it has blinded us to a fact that should never be forgotten — that Jesus was the brother of everybody.

Christianity has often been conceived as a religion that is interested chiefly in the outcasts of society, in the poor, the sick, the depraved. There are many who always think of Jesus as the friend of poor men, and of sick men, and of bad men, who never think of him as the brother of those that are rich and strong and good. It should never be forgotten that Jesus was brotherly toward good men as well as bad men, rich men as well as poor men, respectable men as well as disreputable men — he was the brother of every man. For instance, a rich man in Jericho once climbed into a tree in order to see the prophet pass. Jesus at once told him to come down, and that he wanted to take dinner with him. On a certain occasion near the end of his life, while he sat at meat in the home of one of his friends, a member of the household poured five hundred dollars' worth of ointment on his feet and head, giving us proof that the family was by no means poor. If more is said in the New Testament about poor men than rich men, it is because Jesus was able to come nearer to poor men than he was to rich men. Rich men are always inaccessible. Here in New York you can go into the homes of the poor anywhere, but from the homes of the rich you are barred out. Rich men always surround themselves by barriers, by cordons of servants, and therefore we must not be surprised that in Palestine it was necessary for this man of Galilee to deal largely with the poor.

But it must not be forgotten that he was just as friendly toward the rich Nicodemus as he was to the poor woman at the well; that he was just as brotherly toward rich Zaccheus as he was to the poor beggar in Jerusalem. Nor was he lacking in brotherly interest in the respectable people of his day. If the New Testament makes the impression on us that he was more interested in the outcast and debased, it is because this interest in them was so exceptional that it made a greater impression upon those who wrote the story of his life than any other feature of his conduct. A very large part of all his work was done for respectable people, good people, the leading people of his day. The pious Hebrews of Palestine were tied hand and foot with the cords of tradition. They were bound round and round with laws like an Egyptian mummy with embalming cloths, but Jesus gave himself to the work of setting them free. The cords were tied tight and he attempted to untie the knots, but in his effort to give men emancipation he stirred up animosities and awakened hatreds which led speedily to his death. It was in his effort to untie the knots that men seized him, crying, "Crucify him!"

Let us notice a few illustrations of his brotherliness. When John the Baptist was baptizing in the Jordan, Jesus came down from Galilee to be baptized. John, when he saw Jesus approaching, cried out: "O, no, I cannot baptize you, you are too good. There is reason why I should be baptized of you. This baptism is intended for sinners. I will not, therefore, baptize you." But Jesus would not listen to him, he insisted upon being baptized. He would identify himself with his brethren. "I want to be counted," he said, "a man among men." It was not a question whether he was good or not, it was a question of being brotherly. He refused to hold aloof from any movement that promised good to his country. He subjected himself to the same ceremony of which his fellow-citizens were in need. He took his place at the very beginning of his ministry among his brethren. Nowhere does his brotherliness come out more clearly than in his treatment of the sick. He could not pass a sick man without his soul going out to help him. Pain in its every form appealed to him, misery drew virtue from his heart. A large proportion of all the recorded miracles are miracles of healing. He could not look upon the deaf or dumb, the palsied, the blind, without putting forth his power to help them. No finer illustration of this brotherliness is afforded in the New Testament than that which St. John gives in the story of the impotent man at Bethesda. Here was an invalid who for thirty-eight years had lain in helplessness without a friend in all that great city. He needed only a lift in order to bring him within the reach of influences that were healing, but no one would lend a lifting hand. No other incident in the Bible throws such a strong light upon the inhumanity of the world nineteen hundred years ago. We are living in a day when the spirit of Jesus is working everywhere. Everywhere there is an outstretched hand, and everywhere human hearts are beating in sympathy with the helpless and the sick. Travelers through the Orient tell us that we people of the West have no conception of the indifference of the Oriental heart to human woes and miseries. Jesus, by being brotherly, has set an example after which the life of the world is being patterned, and in every land through which his name has been carried the hearts of men are gentler and their hands more eager to render help.

His brotherliness is also manifested in his teaching. He could not look into men's faces without being pained by their confusion, their perplexity, and their misery. He could not see men passing on to the judgment day without telling them something about the great God in whose world they were living. Whenever he saw men fainting and scattered abroad like sheep having no shepherd, his heart was moved with compassion on them. When he looked into the tired faces of the Galilean peasants his heart cried out, "Come unto me all ye that labor and are heavy laden, and I will give you rest." What a sob there is in the words, "O Jerusalem! Jerusalem!" There is in the words the moan of a brotherly heart. And not only was he brotherly himself, but to him brotherliness is the very essence of religion. Without brotherliness there can be no religion that is pleasing unto God. The old law had said that one man must not kill another, but Jesus went far beyond the requirements of that law — he said that calling a man names was also wicked and would bring him into judgment. To use adjectives that pierce and cut, to throw out mean epithets full of contumely and scorn, to speak of men in ways that degrade them — that is wickedness and will bring the severest retribution. One of the greatest of his parables is the parable of Dives and Lazarus. A rich man fares sumptuously every day, and at his gate there lies a poor sick beggar, his body covered with ulcers, with no friend to bring relief. Only the dogs that prowl the streets lick the loathsome man's sores. Jesus says when that thing happens in this world, something happens in the next world. You can almost feel the heat of his indignant soul. You can hear him asking, "Do you suppose that inhumanity like that will go unpunished in the universe of God?" It was not because the rich man was rich and dressed in fine raiment and fared sumptuously every day, that later on he lifted up his eyes in torment. Abraham also was rich and fared sumptuously every day, but Abraham went to heaven because he had a brother's heart. This rich man Dives went to hell because his heart was not tender, his sympathy did not go out to a brother's need.

And how did Palestine receive this brotherliness? It did not like it. Jesus was too brotherly, men misunderstood him. They misinterpreted him, they maligned him, they laid their plans to kill him; but they could not make him anything else than brotherly. In spite of all their ugliness and vindictiveness he went on helping them all he could, and when they laid their plots to kill him, he went bravely forward giving help, saying: "If I cannot help them with my life I will help them with my death. By dying I will convince them that I wanted to do them good. I, if I be lifted up, will draw all men unto me. When hanging on the cross they will understand me as they cannot understand me now. When they hear me praying for them with my dying breath, they will be convinced that I am indeed their brother."

XIII: THE OPTIMISM OF JESUS

"Be of good cheer."
— John xvi: 33.

By optimism is not meant that jaunty, brainless, happy-go-lucky buoyancy which so often calls itself by this pretentious name. If you insist upon defining an optimist as a man who plays only with sunbeams, and who can hear nothing but harmonies, and who is slightly concerned with the world's agonies and tragedies because of his fancy that no matter what he or any one else does everything is certain to come out all right, then Jesus was not an optimist. There is a sentimental optimism which is irrational and immoral. It is the product of a shallow brain and a stupid heart. It shuts its eyes to all hideous facts and stops its ears to all horrible sounds, and insists that in spite of appearances all is well with the world. This sort of optimism faces the future with a confidence born not of courage but of moral indolence. It assumes that there is in the nature of things an irresistible tendency upward, and that irrespective of the conduct of any man or any set of men, all will be well in the end. No such optimism as this is known in the New Testament.

If we have our superficial optimists, we have also our shallow and short-sighted pessimists. There are men who have a genius for seeing shadows. Their ears are keen for discords. They keep their eyes wide open and see in a lurid light the tragedy of the world's life. Its masses of suffering and wretchedness and woe, its sorrows and vices and sins, lie like a great weight upon the mind and the heart until the former is dizzy and the latter is sick. These men listen to the world's sighing and sobbing and agonizing until history seems a hideous nightmare and existence itself a curse. If such a man were to speak to you to-night, he would tell you a story which would lacerate and darken your heart. He would remind you of what the thieves and the robbers, big and little, have been doing. He would call your attention to the stories of greed and lust, cruelty and lawlessness, which have recently come in from all parts of the world. He would pile up before you the sickening record of a single month's outrage and atrocity and crime, and then ask you if it is not clear that everything is going to the dogs. These pessimists lift up their voices on every side. They tell us that republican institutions are in a process of decay, that our cities are hopelessly corrupted and sunken, that the days of the republic itself are numbered. As for society there is no health in it. From its head to its feet there is nothing but festering sores. Babylon never matched our luxury, and Rome never touched the depths of our infamy. The church like everything else is decaying and is fit only for the bonfire. We may whistle if we wish to keep up our courage; but after us — the deluge! The world is running down a very steep place toward the edge of the abyss. Not a few men are thus thinking and speaking. Two of the greatest writers of the nineteenth century, Thomas Carlyle and John Ruskin, were pessimistic in their temper and outlook. The Scotchman filled the world with his shriekings and the Englishman filled the world with his sighings. Innumerable smaller men are filling the world with their sniffiings and whimperings. But from the grinning optimist and the hysterical pessimist, we can expect little. They have nothing to offer toward the solution of the great world problems.

Let us open our New Testament and listen to a man who in these confused and distracting times can give us confidence and hope. Jesus of Nazareth was not a man who could shut his eyes to the sorrow and the heart-break of the world. Never were eyes wider open than his. He saw everything. He saw things which the world had passed by unnoticed. He saw suffering in its every form — it tugged at his heart strings. The tired, sad faces of human beings haunted him, they spoke to him of the tragedy of the world's disordered heart. He had ears which caught every shriek of agony, every cry of distress, every sigh of want. He saw with eyes which pierced. Underneath the tragedy of suffering he saw the blacker tragedy of sin. Down underneath the surface of the world's life he saw the cancer which was eating up its strength and its hope and its joy. He recognized as none other the tremendous power of evil. He saw with open eyes the roads which lead to death. He knew, as no other has ever known so well, that evil must be resisted, that sin must be faced and grappled with, that it is only by struggle, suffering, and death that the victory can be won. But he remains nevertheless undaunted. He never loses heart. He sees all, and he hears all, but he never gives up hope. He faces facts as they are, and he predicts grander facts which are to be. He sees both sides — the bright side and the dark side — and having seen both sides his face has light on it. He sings and he also sobs. His singing is sometimes broken by his sobbing, but he is never overwhelmed, he never surrenders, his head is always up, and his unfailing exhortation is, "Be of good cheer!"

This is the dominating note of the New Testament. It comes up out of the heart of the blackest tragedy which our world has known. What a sad and depressing book the New Testament ought to be considering the dismal story it has to tell! It gives us the life of one who was a man of sorrows and acquainted with grief. It portrays his sufferings through the cruel, disappointing years to his horrible death upon the cross. It narrates his awful predictions of coming woe and loss and ruin. It tells us that the leading cities of Galilee are rushing to destruction, and that even Jerusalem, glorious with the triumphs of a thousand years, is irretrievably doomed and that not one stone of all its stately edifices shall be left standing on another. Its destruction shall be complete. And yet notwithstanding this heart-breaking story, the New Testament does not depress us or leave a shadow on the heart. It is a jubilant, exhilarating book, and the words which linger longest in the ear are, "Be of good cheer, I have overcome the world." The New Testament is a gospel, a bit of glorious news, because at the centre of it there lives and works the world's greatest optimist.

Here is the optimist whom we have been looking for. This is the man who can inspire our confidence and give us hope. We need a man with open eye and open ear and open heart, a man who sees things as they are and knows the thickness of the belt of night. We cannot follow a leader who keeps crying, "Peace," when we know that there is no peace; nor can we trust a teacher who asserts that all is well, when his assertion is contradicted daily by the experience of the world. Give us a man who feels the fury of the storm, and is also certain of the calm which is going to follow. Give us a man who can measure accurately the dimensions of the night, and who also sees the dawning of a glorious morning. Jesus is the prince of optimists — his optimism is the optimism of God Himself.

Let us try to find the secret of Jesus' optimism. The secret is written large across the pages of the Gospel. It was a secret too good to keep — he gave it to everybody who had ears to hear. It was an abiding confidence in God. We are sure of Him sometimes. Our faith is clouded and it is intermittent. It floods and ebbs like the tide. Jesus never doubted. His vision was unclouded. His trust was absolute. To him God was an everpresent Father. This was his new name for God. The prophets and poets of Israel had only seldom ventured to think of God as father, and then only by way of dim surmise. With Jesus, God was always Father. This is the name he carried on his lips when a boy of twelve, it was on his lips when he passed from this world into the other. He placed it on the lips of every man who followed him. It constantly amazed him that men had so little faith in God. "Have faith in God!" This was the exhortation with which he braced the hearts of those who wished to live his life and do his work. The words came with the power of a revelation, because warm with the blood of a heart which knew the secret of perfect trust.

Along with unswerving trust in God there went an unshakable confidence in man. Jesus believed in human nature. He saw the possibilities and capacities of the human heart. He saw men's littlenesses, frailties, vices, sins, but underneath all these he saw a soul created in God's image. The deepest thing in man he saw to be not animalism but Godlikeness. He called Simon the son of Jonas a rock, when Simon was counted the most fickle and fluctuating man in all the town. Jesus saw that which was deepest in him. He had confidence not only in people who went to church, but also in people who never went. He had hope of the Publicans and sinners. He knew that Zaccheus could repent and that Matthew could become a preacher. He believed that men and women who have fallen all the way to the bottom can climb back again, "The harlots are going into the kingdom before you!" — thus he spoke to a company of hardhearted pessimists who had lost confidence in the recoverableness of human nature. Man, in spite of his aberrations and stumblings and fallings, is a being on whom you can rely, he has in him the very essence and nature of God. And so Jesus said to Simon Peter, "Thou art rock and upon this rock I will build my church, and the gates of Hades shall not prevail against it!" What sublime confidence! Can an unconquerable institution, one against which no forces in the universe can possibly prevail, be constructed out of men? Can impregnable walls be built of human nature? Can eternal foundations be laid in human hearts? Yes, says Jesus, and without a doubt of the fidelity of his apostles, he rolled the huge world upon their shoulders and went away.

Nor could any experience break down this trust in the divine capacities of human nature. When has a man had greater reason to abandon faith in men than this optimist of Galilee? He lived in a corrupt and demoralizing age. Government was both tyrannical and rotten. Its officials were for the most part cynics and grafters. The Jewish church was formal, lifeless, and hypocritical. Its leaders, many of them, were dead to the movements of

God's spirit. Society was disgustingly corrupt. Men had grown sceptical everywhere of the honesty of man or the virtue of woman. But Jesus trusted men. He did this in the teeth of experiences which swept over him like a dark and devastating flood. His entire career was a tragedy. He was suspected, misrepresented, hated. He was surrounded by liars wherever he went. No matter what he said his sentences were twisted, and no matter what he did his motives were impugned. Such treatment is apt to sour the heart of any one who is long subjected to it. Jesus was mistreated all the way. The inhuman wretches who tortured him in the courtyard of Pontius Pilate were doing only what men had done to him from the beginning. His life was one long-drawn crucifixion. Men were always jamming thorns into his brow, jabbing spears into his side, driving spikes through his hands and feet. But he never gave up faith in human nature. When he saw that men were determined to take his life he said, "If I be lifted up, I will draw all men unto me!" He felt that no matter what cruel and devilish things human nature might be guilty of, there was after all down deep in the heart that which would respond to forgiveness and love. The enemies of Jesus were the meanest, most unprincipled, diabolical set of human hounds which ever tracked an innocent man to death; but they never broke down his confidence in the divinity of the human heart.

It was not only his enemies but his friends who caused him unspeakable anguish. Among his own disciples, in the innermost circle of his trusted friends, there was a man who in return for all his confidence and all his goodness became a traitor, and betrayed him into the hands of the men who had agreed upon his death. And this traitor did not betray him in a manner decent even among traitors, but in a way of which a devil might have been ashamed. He betrayed Jesus with a kiss. Hell itself can produce nothing viler than sugar-coated treachery. But no matter what individual men may do, man is to be trusted still. When he comes to his true self, he will say, "I will arise and go to my Father!"

The faith of Jesus is in marked contrast to the scepticism of many individuals whom we have known. There is nothing so staggering to one's confidence in human nature as an unfortunate experience in early life. A young man starts out, hopeful and trustful, falls in with men of good reputation and high standing who gouge him and skin him, and for the rest of his life the man is sceptical and possibly cynical. A young woman begins life with a heart which trusts everybody. She is deceived and betrayed, either by man or by woman, and she carries a wound which time does not heal. There are in every community men and women, soured on the world, suspicious of everybody, clinging to the conviction that there is nobody in whom one can trust. Would that all such cynics might come to Jesus and learn from him to expect large things from human nature everywhere. He sees the shallowness, the paltriness, the frailty of the heart; but he also sees its capacities, its possibilities, the mustard-seed germs of virtues and graces which the Spirit of God can unfold. We measure men too much by their powers, and not enough by their capacities, by what they are to-day and not by what they may become later on. It was because the eyes of Jesus swept the future that he could stand around the wreckage of a race in ruins and say, "Be of good cheer!"

This indomitable Optimist has confidence in you. You have no hope for yourself. He has. You see your weakness, sordidness, vileness; he sees deeper, and seeing deeper he has hope for you. He sees your capacity of God. He knows what you can do when you have come to yourself. He sees deeper also into God. You have no adequate conception of the patience or the mercy of the Infinite Father. He has. You do not know what Infinite Love can accomplish. He does. Because of your transgressions you have lost faith in yourself. He has not. Because you have failed a thousand times you say there is no use trying any more. He says, "Try again!" If you give yourself to him, he will make of you an optimist"

XIV: THE CHIVALRY OF JESUS

"And touched him."
— Matthew viii: 3.

I HAVE found difficulty in finding a word to express the quality of Jesus to which I now desire to invite your attention. This quality is courage, but it is something more than courage. Courage is a temper of the heart, a firmness of spirit in the presence of difficulty and danger. But there are many kinds of courage. There is first of all bravery, an intrepid sort of courage which has in it a certain daring which ordinary courage does not have. Bravery steps ahead of courage and takes risks which the latter does not invite. Moreover there is fortitude or courage in its passive form. If bravery rushes forward to attack, fortitude holds its ground and endures. And then again there is valor which we have consecrated for service on the battlefield, and gallantry which is an adventurous and splendid variety of heroism — heroism as it were with a halo. But not one of these words is rich or wide enough to express all that is in my mind when I contemplate a certain side of the courageous heart of Jesus. He was heroic but he was more than that. His heroism was a superb gallantry and something more. There was in it a delicious courtesy, a beautiful and gentle graciousness toward the weak and helpless. Possibly we can find no better word to cover this rich characteristic of the heart of Jesus than the word "chivalry." It is a word taken from the world of knighthood. The very sound of the word has magic in it, and calls up before the eyes splendid troops of heroic men who went forth in the mediaeval times to protect the weak, maintain the right, and live a stainless life. In a world from which justice had been largely banished and in which might had usurped the place of right, the knight arose to defend the weak and to bring just causes through to victory. Woman especially was the object of his care. By her weakness she appealed to that which was deepest in his heart. By defending her and all others who like her were at the mercy of the brute powers of a barbaric world the knight won for himself a shining place in history and gave to chivalry a splendor which will never fade. Jesus of Nazareth was a knight. On foot he travelled forth, clad in the armor of a peerless manhood, to shield the weak, maintain the right, and live a life which should charm and win the world. At the head of the great company of knightly souls by whose bravery and prowess the world has been made better, stands this knight of knights, this chivalric Man of Galilee.

His gracious courage first manifested itself at the river Jordan on the day on which he was baptized. John did not want to baptize him. There was no reason why he should be baptized. His heart was unstained by sin and the baptism of John was a baptism of repentance. To be baptized, therefore, might lead to misunderstandings and give rise to misrepresentations. There were many risks in this yielding of himself to baptism, but he accepted them all because his great soul yearned to identify himself with his countrymen, with the common race of men. Men were sinners, they needed repentance, they needed just the baptism to which the prophet of the desert was calling them, and this young carpenter from Nazareth, with no need in his own soul for the baptismal water, goes bravely forward saying, "I too must be baptized." Strong himself, he will identify himself with this reformatory movement. Lifted above the sins of ordinary humanity he will link himself at the very start with those who carry on their hearts the burden of transgression and who cry out day and night for deliverance. A knight he was at the beginning; a knight he will be to the end.

Mark how his soul goes out to those who suffer. Physical distress pierced him and wrung his heart. Sickness in the first century did not receive the attention which it receives in ours. The poor were allowed to suffer unattended and to die unrelieved. There were no hospitals such as ours, and no earnest bands of philanthropic men and women giving their lives to the alleviation of pain and to banishing the terrors of the dying hour. Insane people were not housed and cared for. Supposed to be possessed by devils, they were driven out of the town and allowed to wander in cemeteries and desert places, a terror to all who heard their shrieks and cries. Jesus pitied them. No one else reached out to them a helping hand. The Evangelists take delight in telling us how again and again he healed those who were afflicted with demons. If there was a man in Palestine more dreaded than a maniac it was a leper. But even the leper was not beyond the reach of Jesus' heart. Men turned their backs upon him. Laws prescribed the distance which he must keep from every other human being. Between him and all others there was a deep gulf fixed, but this Knight of Nazareth crossed the chasm and to the consternation of all Palestine not only spoke kindly to the leper, but laid his hand upon him.

His heart was ever open to the neglected and forlorn. Between Galilee and Judea there lived a tribe of people, half Jewish and half Pagan, who in their religion as well as in their blood exhibited a degeneration from the high ideals of the early times. Degenerates and apostates, they were held in deep abhorrence by Hebrews whose hearts were true to the high traditions of their country. It was only in cases of necessity that a Jew could be induced to pass through the region inhabited by these people. Jesus not only passed through Samaria, but he tarried there and taught the people just as he taught the men of Judea and Galilee. They were outcasts, but they were also human, and if they had no protector or friend, he at any rate would befriend them. Some of them might not understand how to receive him, but such churlish conduct could not dampen the ardor of his interest in them. The disciples with blazing hearts might want to bum up a Samaritan village, but the Knight of Galilee came not to destroy but to save. No man could take his place on the side of the Samaritans without paying an awful penalty, and Jesus paid it. Men gnashed their teeth and hissed, "You are a Samaritan." That was the most cutting thing it was possible for them to say, but he never swerved from his course. He healed Samaritan lepers as freely as any others, and when he painted a man who represented his ideal of goodness he painted him with the features and dress of a Samaritan. The parable which has probably taken the deepest hold on the heart of the world of all the parables which Jesus spoke is the parable of the "Good Samaritan." The creation of that parable was a sublime act of chivalry.

There were outcasts even in Galilee and Judea. There were people who were estranged from organized religion. They neglected the observances and regulations of the synagogue, and were labelled "sinners" by the pious. They were not in all cases profligates or vagabonds, but simply men and women who had no liking for the ceremonies of the church and who took no interest in the Rabbis or their teachings. The Rabbis in return took no interest in them. They were counted renegades and apostates, from whose society it was well that all decent people should hold aloof. In many of these people there were aspirations after better things, and in all of them there were the deep hungers and warm feelings of our common humanity. But they were outcasts. The church had laid a ban upon them. They were dangerous. Their example was demoralizing, their ideas were poison. No one who cared for his reputation as a God-fearing man dared to associate with them. No Rabbi in all Palestine would risk his good name by dining with any one of them. But Jesus was not a man to be deterred by the execrations of polite society. The so-called sinners were human beings, and because children of God they were not to be despised. If no other religious teacher would go among them, he would. He did. He made himself of no reputation. He sat down with sinners and ate with them. The Pharisees never forgave him. His courtesy to the unchurched masses hastened the day of his crucifixion.

Among the so-called sinners there was a group of men lower than all the others, known as Publicans. These were tax collectors whose business it was to collect Jewish money and send it up to Rome. The tax collector is never a popular personage, and if he collects money to send to an outside and tyrannical power he is not only unpopular but execrated. The Publicans of Palestine were hated with a fury of detestation which modern society cannot parallel. Publicans were counted lower than street dogs. The Jewish church would not allow them even to contribute to its treasury. But Jesus made friends of these men. They were friendless, and in many cases of unsavory character, but he was a physician, and like all true physicians he was especially interested in those who were dangerously ill. Not only did he go into their homes and eat with them in a cosmopolitan city like Capernaum, but he dined with a prominent leader of the Publicans in the old priestly city of Jericho. Not only did he eat with them, but when the time came to select twelve men who should be his most intimate friends and most conspicuous workers, one of them was a Publican. And then as if to push his chivalry to a climax he painted a picture of two men praying in the temple — one a Pharisee and the other a Publican. One need not wonder that the Pharisees cried: "Crucify him! Crucify him!" When was a knight ever so reckless in throwing his protection round the weak?

But as is the case with all true knights, it is in his attitude to woman that Jesus' chivalry reaches its finest expression. Woman has never been fairly treated in the Orient. She has always been counted inferior to man. Sometimes she has been a toy, most frequently a drudge, and always something a little higher than an animal but far lower than a man. The degradation of woman in such countries as India, for example, is a shock and a bewilderment to all observing travellers. The Hindu treatment of woman is a tragedy the full blackness of which has never been realized by the people of the West. Those who best understand the Indian problem assert that there is no hope for India until woman is given there her rightful place. It is with such facts in mind that we are able to appreciate the grotesque folly and the ludicrous ignorance of those American women who have an inextinguishable craving for the religions of the distant East. These women, not satisfied with Christianity, and being somewhat weary of the teachings of Jesus, sit spellbound at the feet of sundry Hindu teachers, who without authority or standing in their own country come to America to expound the beautiful ideas of Oriental religion. These teachers have much to say in poetic phrases about ideas exquisitely nebulous, and conceptions which are so vague that they cannot be grasped even by the minds to which they bring rapture, but they have nothing to say about the place of woman as that place is taught in orthodox Hinduism or as that place is established in the best Hindu society. It is both farcical and pathetic — this trailing of American women after these Eastern teachers, and the quickest way to end it is to let the West know just what India has to teach and show in regard to the place and rights of woman. It is amazing that any informed man should ever leave Jesus for any other teacher, but it is tenfold more astounding that any woman in her right mind should ever turn her back on the one man who has done more for woman than all the other men who have ever lived. Of all the knights who have risked their lives for the protection and honor of womanhood not one is worthy to unloose the latchet of the shoes of this gracious and gallant Man of Galilee. How boldly he spoke on the subject of divorce. Woman's position in Palestine was superior to that of woman in surrounding nations, but even in Palestine she was at the mercy of the man. A man could divorce his wife when he chose, and all that the law required was that he should write out a statement declaring that whereas this woman was once his wife she was now his wife no longer.

But against such arbitrary and dangerous authority the chivalric soul of Jesus protested. Men reminded him that such liberty had been granted to man by Moses, but he immediately replied that Moses would never have allowed any such license had he not been dealing with barbarians, and that no matter what Moses or any other lawmaker had ever said or decreed, the law of God is that a man has no right to cast a woman off as soon as he is tired of her. Marriage is ordained by God. It lies in the very structure and formation of human nature. The union is not one which can be dissolved by Moses or anybody else. God intends that one man shall live with one woman and that they shall live together until death parts them. No greater words than those have ever been spoken on behalf of woman since the world began. Even now men's hearts are too hard to hear and heed them, and the result is degradation, heartbreak, and misery. High above all the clamorous voices of the world there rings the clear and authoritative tone of Jesus saying to men: "You have no right to use women and toss them from you. Man and woman belong together, and after marriage the twain are one flesh."

There were many degraded women in Palestine as there are to-day in America. Woman being weaker than man is the first to suffer from the injustices of every social and economic system. Our modern world has created a dozen places for women where one place existed in the olden world. Unable to earn their livelihood by honest means women then, as women now, became the prey of brutal men. And men then, as some men now, insisted on two standards of morality, — one for men and one for women, the second standard being higher than the first. One of these degraded women was caught one day by a lot of men who dragged her into the presence of Jesus just to see what he would say and do. According to the Palestinian law a woman guilty of adultery could be stoned to death. As soon as the men had made their accusation, Jesus paused a moment and then said, "The man among you who has not committed the same sin may throw the first stone." Not a stone was lifted. No one said a word. Those who were on the outskirts of the crowd one by one disappeared. By and by they all had gone. All had slunk away like curs. Woman is not to be condemned and man let go free. In the scales of God's eternal justice a woman's sin is not heavier than that of a man. Here is a teacher who does not hesitate to defend the rights of woman even though by so doing he incurs the deadly hatred of all foul-hearted men. Even women of the street shall not be denied the privilege of repentance, for they are capable of remorse, and may long to find their way back to the Father's house. A woman has a mind, a conscience, a soul, even though she lives in Samaria and has broken the moral law, and is worthy of careful instruction at the hands of the greatest of teachers. What a piece of gallantry it was — that conversation at Jacob's well!

Here, then, we have a knight who is a knight indeed. The mediaeval knight went forth seeking for adventures: our knight of Palestine went forth in search of forlorn and friendless human beings. The knight of France and Germany was clad in metal, this knight of Nazareth had no protection but the white innocence of an unspoiled heart. His was the skill of a physician and not that of a soldier. His was the prowess of a friend and brother and not that of a warrior fighting to lay his antagonist in the dust. He had all the graces and virtues of mediaeval chivalry and none of its superficiality or its foibles. He had the nerve, the mettle, and the intrepidity of the bravest of the knights, and along with this he had a sweet winsomeness, a divine graciousness which history cannot match. Many a knight protected the distressed and maintained the right but failed to live the stainless life. This prince of knights, this king of all the hosts of chivalry, conquered on every field and came off without a stain.

He liked people. He was interested in human beings. He loved a crowd. The populace appealed to him. The masses were dear to his heart. Ignorant people attracted him. Bewildered and mistaken people had a fascination for him. Wicked people had a place in his heart. He could not look at a great crowd without feeling the tragedy of human life and crying out: "Come unto me! Come unto me!" His invitations were always generous. They were wide enough to cover all. He always said that no man who came would ever be cast out.

In Jesus we have a revelation of the heart of God. In speaking of the chivalry of this man of Nazareth I have been speaking of the chivalry of the Eternal. God is knightly in His disposition, chivalric in His temper. It is His work from all eternity to protect the weak, maintain the right, and live a stainless life. His heart goes out unceasingly toward the weak, the helpless, and those who have no friend. If you are conscious of your weakness, cry out to Him, for He is swift to answer such a cry. If you feel sometimes absolutely helpless, altogether forlorn and forsaken, do not despair, for the heart of Jesus is the heart which beats in and behind all this world, and you can never be forsaken so long as God is God. In your moments of depression and in the days when the world seems cold and cruel, think of the chivalric God, whose heart beats in sympathy with weakness, and who goes out with alacrity and with gladness to meet every soul in need of succor.

XV: THE FIRMNESS OF JESUS

"Get thee behind me, Satan."
— Matthew xvi: 23.

Let us think to-night of the firmness of Jesus. Of his tenderness we think often, and also of his gentleness and graciousness. To these lovely graces the heart is joyfully responsive, and in dwelling upon them we are likely to overlook other traits no less beautiful and praiseworthy. Gentleness of nature is not a virtue but a defect unless it is accompanied by tenacity of will. Sweetness of disposition is not enough to make a man useful and noble. Along with the sweetness there must go strength, and underneath the moods soft as velvet there must lie a resoluteness hard as steel.

The weakness of men under the play of social forces is one of the outstanding tragedies of history. To build a will strong enough to resist and control these forces is the central and crucial task of education. It is an ancient adage that evil companionships corrupt good morals. All men are more or less moulded by the society of which they form a part. The child yields readily to the ideas and habits of his fellows, and no matter what his ancestry may have been, his environment if corrupt may bring him speedily to ruin. This impressionability is not a trait peculiar to childhood, but is carried with us through every stage of life. The young man in college is powerfully influenced by those of his classmates who are the nearest to him, and sometimes a few bold, masterful spirits will set the pace for a thousand men. Business men are as susceptible as college students and yield in crowds to the influence of a few dominating minds. The slavery of the social world has long been a theme for moralists and satirists. He is indeed a strong character who dares run counter to the traditions and fashions of the world in which he moves. Even the strongest and most independent often bow down before standards against which conscience revolts and submit to customs against which the heart protests. Humanity goes in crowds and droves, and no bondage is too absurd or galling to be submitted to. The majority of mortals are not strong enough to be themselves: they become echoes of their neighbors and walk in paths marked out by others. There is a spirit of the age which leaves its impress on every mind. Even the mightiest men cannot free themselves entirely from it. As Lowell says, "Every man is the prisoner of his date." We apologize for Cromwell and Calvin and Luther and Hildebrand and Augustine, saying, "Remember the times in which they lived!"

But when we come to Jesus of Nazareth we are in the presence of a man whom nobody swerved or dominated, who is so free from the bias of his race and so clean of the spirit of his age that he seems to belong to all races and all ages. He is not the Son of David but the Son of Man, just genuinely, supremely human. He is not a citizen of the first century only, but the contemporary of each succeeding generation. Immersed in an ocean of mighty forces which beat upon him furiously through every hour of his career, he resisted them all successfully by the indomitable energy of a victorious will, living a life unique in its beauty and achieving a work unmarred by the limitations either of time or place. That he was not insensible to the dominant forces of his time, he himself has told us in the story of the temptation. His countrymen had formed definite ideas of the Messiah. He was to be a wonder worker and the manifestations of his power were to be spectacular and overwhelming. He was to trample opposing forces under his feet and make Palestine the centre of the world. This was the dream, this was the expectation. The best men expected this, as did also the worst men. It is a dangerous thing to baffle popular expectations. It is almost cruel to extinguish the fire of a nation's hope. Good and great men have found no difficulty in every land and generation in bringing themselves to yield, at least up to a certain point, to the wishes and demands of their countrymen. It all seems plausible enough. The argument is familiar, for we have heard it even in the present generation. Who is a man that he should set himself against the expressed wish of a nation? Is it not through the people that God makes his wishes known, and what is it but egotism or insanity which would lead an individual to set his judgment against the judgment of the people? This is the argument whose sharp edge many a leader has felt, and Jesus of Nazareth felt it too. Wherever he went he heard the people clamoring for a king, a king who should rise to supremacy over the wrecked empire of Caesar. The nation was ripe for revolution. A word from him would, like a spark, have kindled a mighty conflagration. Expectations had been built up by men anointed by Jehovah, and these expectations were glowing hot, and how could Jesus hope to win the attention of his people or control the current of their life unless he fell in with their ideals and attempted to carry out the program on which their hearts were set? It was a great temptation, so terrific that he told his apostles all about it. He assured them that in this temptation he had been wrestling with the very prince of infernal powers, but that notwithstanding repeated assaults he had come out of the conflict victorious. In choosing the road which led to supremacy by way of Gethsemane and Golgotha, he renounced the ideals of his countrymen and disappointed their dearest expectations, but so firm was he that the hosts of hell speaking through God's chosen people could not move him from his place. The nation hurled itself with frantic force against him, but he did not budge. He was the Rock of Ages.

When we study his life with attentive eyes we see it was one long resistance to the forces of his age. He was a patriot, but he could not go with his countrymen in any of their patriotic programs or expectations. He was a churchman, but he could not go with the members of the Jewish church in their favorite teachings and ceremonies. The religious teachers taught doctrines of the Sabbath which he could not accept. They presented forms of worship which he could not submit to. They laid down lines of separation which it was impossible for him to observe. It is not easy to run counter to the deep-seated feelings of the most religious people of one's day, or to cut across the grain of the prejudices of the most conscientious men in the town. There were many reasons why Jesus should have conformed to the ideas and customs of the church, but he firmly resisted all the voices which urged him toward conformity, standing out alone in defiance of what the best men were doing and saying, notwithstanding his nonconformity seemed to the majority impiety and to many blasphemy. For a godly man to be classed among blasphemers is one of the bitterest experiences which the heart can know. But Jesus paid the price and continued firm.

Men of light and leading have an influence surpassing that of ordinary men. There were men in Palestine who by learning and position had won the confidence and esteem of their countrymen. As leaders and teachers of the people they had their plans and systems and into these they attempted to work this young man from Galilee. They recognized in him a man of force, and to manipulate him and make use of him was a natural ambition. No man with a noble cause to promote will lightly antagonize the most influential men of his day. He will bend to them so far as he is able, he will yield to their whims and caprices so far as conscience will permit, he will go with them so far as this is possible; but if he is a man of strength, he will not compromise his principles, and he will never jeopardize the victory of his cause by playing into the hands of men whose faces are toward a different goal. Jesus could not be manipulated. He refused to be used. One party after another tried to work him into its scheme, but he was incorrigibly intractable and went on his way independent, unshackled, free. All the seductions offered by the men who sat on thrones could not swerve him from his course, and although his steadfastness made him enemies and finally nailed him to the cross, he was everywhere and always a man who could not be moved.

There are men who are too strong to be manipulated by their foes, but in the hands of their friends they are plastic as wax. Jesus could not be manipulated even by his friends. He had many friends in Nazareth, but he never gave up his principles to please them. They had their prejudices and superstitions, but he never surrendered to them. He knew their bigotry and narrowness, and so in his opening sermon he read the story of God's compassion on a Syrian leper, and also on a Sidonian widow. His sermon raised the storm which he had anticipated, but he bore the fury of it without flinching. He would not keep silence when he knew he ought to speak, nor would he turn aside from the path he knew he ought to travel even though by sticking to the path he made himself a lifelong exile. The respect and good-will of neighbors are sweet indeed, but these must not be bought by bending.

But probably no neighbor in Nazareth was ever so near to Jesus' heart as his dear friend Simon Peter. At a crisis in Jesus' life Peter did his best to dissuade him from a certain course, but the loyal and loving friend succeeded no better than the most hostile Pharisee. This man of Nazareth could not be moved by friend or foe. It was his Father's business he was attending to, and therefore all efforts to draw him aside were made in vain. "Get thee behind me, Satan," he said to the astonished Peter, recognizing in him the same evil spirit he had contended with years before in the desert. To defy the threats of powerful enemies is hard, but to turn a deaf ear to the expostulations of loving friends is harder still. Only a man of unconquerable will is equal to a test so taxing. Jesus met it and did not fail.

It was a test he faced in his own home. His brothers did not understand him. Their lack of understanding curtailed their sympathy with him. From their standpoint he often did the injudicious thing, and refused to do the thing which would have forwarded his reputation. They were always ready with advice. He could not take it. They urged him to go to Jerusalem at a time when he could not go. They exhorted him to go home at a time when his duty was to be somewhere else. Only a man who has been driven by conscience to go contrary to the wishes of members of his own family can enter into the experience which Jesus suffered or can measure the strength of will which one must have to resist successfully the importunities of love.

This test of will power reached its climax in Jesus' conflict with his mother. She loved him and he loved her, but he could not always carry out her wishes. There comes a time in many a man's life when even his own mother's exhortations must go unheeded in order to obey a higher call. Such an experience came to Jesus. It was a sword through Mary's heart, and it was a sword also through the heart of Jesus. The painful experience in the Temple at the age of twelve was probably not the first of the kind in Jesus' life, and it was certainly not the last. The ties to Mary were not so deep as the ties which bound Jesus to the heavenly Father, and when Mary's wish conflicted with the Father's will, the wish of the woman was pushed aside to make room for the will of God.

Here, then, we have a situation which is distressing indeed. The most tender and gracious and obliging of men is compelled to resist not only the prayers of his countrymen but the wishes of his family and friends. He stands like a rock in the midst of a troubled sea, and all its billows dash themselves against his feet in vain. There was something inflexible in his will, something granitic in his soul. When he found a man whom he thought worthy to be the first member of his church he called him "rock." Are we to infer from this that it is the rock-like quality which is indispensable in the building of an institution which shall endure? It is certain that Jesus loved stability in others, and what he loved in others he had superabundantly in himself. Firm himself, he loved men who could not be moved. Unconquerable himself, he intrusted his Gospel to men who would endure and never flinch. Men who having put their hand to the plough looked back were not men he could make use of in the saving of a world. Men who started to build a tower and then gave up the undertaking were only objects of mirth and mockery. Salvation could not be offered to any one who did not endure to the end.

It is in this tenacity of will that we find an indispensable element of Christian character. Men are to resist exterior forces and form their life from within. They are not to be swayed by current opinion, but by the spirit of the Eternal in their heart. They are not to listen to the voices of time, but to live and work for eternity. We like this steadfastness in human character, and we also crave it in God. Men have always loved to think of Him as the unchanging and the unchangeable, the one "with whom can be no variation, neither shadow that is cast by turning." And what we desire in God we find in Jesus of Nazareth. He also is unchanging and unchangeable A writer of the first century encourages the hearts of his readers by reminding them that 'Jesus Christ is the same yesterday and to-day, yea and forever.' Jesus never called himself the Rock, but the Christian heart soon gave him that appellation, and few hymns have proved so popular in the English-speaking world as —

"Rock of Ages, cleft for me!
Let me hide myself in thee."

What Jesus was in Palestine he is to-day and shall be for evermore. All his promises stand unshaken, all his warnings remain unchanged. His attitude to sinners is to-day what it has been from the beginning and what it will be to the end. You cannot discourage him by your ingratitude, you cannot make him other than he is by your disobedience. He is not broken down by human folly or driven from his plan by human perversity. From age to age he is about his Father's business, and in the midst of all nations and kindreds and tongues he goes about doing good.

XVI: THE GENEROSITY OF JESUS

"It is more blessed to give than to receive."
— Acts XX: 35.

Paul is speaking farewell words to the officers of the church to which he has given more time and love than to any other. He reminds them of things he has often said to them before, and in closing calls to their minds one of the most illuminating and helpful of all the sayings of the Master, "It is more blessed to give than to receive." These words express with rare fulness one of the finest of the traits of Jesus, his generosity.

If one were asked to mention a half dozen keywords of Christian duty, he would be sure to place the word "give" high in the list. One cannot read the New Testament without being halted by that word, for it occurs repeatedly, and always with an emphasis which arrests the heart. Indeed, it has been often claimed that the Man of Galilee is wild and reckless in his theory of giving. His saying, "Give to him that asketh thee, and from him that would borrow of thee turn not thou away," has been to many a mystery and an offence. But the exhortation need stagger no one if it is remembered that all action is to be subjected to the limitations of love. Mortals are urged to give as God gives, and God's giving is always fashioned and conditioned by his love. He does not give to every man the precise thing which the man asks for. He says to all of us not once but many times, "No," "no," "no!" Love can never give where giving would work hurt. The mother cannot give the razor to the little girl who pleads for it, nor can the father grant his son every favor which he asks. The man half drunk who begs for a quarter on the street corner must be refused, and in every case the petitioner must be dealt with according to the requirements of the law of love. But to write down all the considerations and qualifications which must be taken into account in dealing with a world which is always asking, was for Jesus a plain impossibility. It was better to throw out the great word "give," unqualified and naked, allowing it to speak unhindered to the human heart, as a word which holds in it a revelation of the mind of God. St. Luke tells us that one day when Jesus was unfolding his idea of generosity, he said: "Give, and it shall be given unto you; good measure, pressed down, and shaken together, and running over shall men give into your bosom. For with the same measure that ye mete withal it shall be measured to you again." To understand this you must have been some time on a farm and watched the farmer measure grains or small fruits. The pressing down and the shaking together and the running over all are graphic and meaningful expressions intended to picture to the mind the kind of measure in which the king of heaven takes delight. A man who does not skimp or dole out with a niggardly hand is, says Jesus, a man whom the universe likes and blesses. He will lose nothing by his liberality, for the world is constructed on a generous principle, and by surrendering himself to the divine spirit of giving he will be in tune with the Infinite, and shall by no means lose his reward. He need not be anxious about the precise time when such action shall bring its recompense. It is enough to go forward, giving and asking nothing in return, assured that somewhere and somehow his recompense shall be forthcoming. Let him therefore when he makes a dinner or supper not invite simply his friends or his brethren, or his kindred or his rich neighbors, expecting that they will invite him again. Let him feast the poor, the maimed, the lame, the blind, men who cannot give anything in return, and then let him expect from God the blessing which is provided for the generous heart. That blessing may not come in all its fulness in the world that now is, but there will be a complete recompense at the resurrection of the just. What Jesus said to his disciples he says to all, "Freely ye have received, freely give."

Jesus' dislike of the stingy and parsimonious heart comes out in several of his parables. When he speaks of Dives in his fine linen at his banquet-table while the sick beggar eats crumbs at his gate, we can feel the hot flame of an indignant soul. When he tells of the rich man who thought of nothing but his overflowing barns and his own selfish enjoyment, there is a scorn in his language which scorches. In the parable of the Hours recorded in the twentieth chapter of Matthew, he passes condemnation on men who are so penurious and mean that the beauty of a generous act does not appeal to them. The owner of the vineyard pays the men who worked longest all that he agreed to pay them, and then because of the generosity of his heart he pays the men who have worked only one hour as much as if they had worked an entire day. He does this because he wants to be generous. But selfish and mole-eyed men began to murmur. An act that should have charmed them by its loveliness excited only their envy and ill-natured grumblings. The story is told in a way which reveals clearly what

Jesus thinks of a man who is generous. Where in the New Testament will you find more exuberant praise than that which he lavishes upon the woman who poured four hundred dollars' worth of perfume on his head and feet? Miserly souls near him were offended by such extravagance, but he liked it. He appreciated the lavish expenditures of love. When he sees a poor widow throwing her two bits of copper into the treasury in the temple, all the money she had in the world, he does not criticise her for doing a foolish thing as most of us would have done, but he cries out in a shout which has in it the music of a hallelujah, "She has given more than they all." In a world so filled with grudging and close-fisted men, it cheered his great heart to see now and then a person who had mastered the divine art of giving. He liked givers because he himself was always giving.

When he said it is more blessed to give than to receive he was speaking from personal experience. He had not read that in a book. He had found it out in life. When he urged men to give freely, abundantly, lavishly, gladly, continually, he was only preaching what he himself practised. He had no money to give, but he gave without stint what he had. He had time and he gave it. The golden hours were his and he gave them. He gave them all. So recklessly did he give them that in order to find time to pray it was necessary to use hours when other men were sleeping. He had strength and he gave it with a liberality which astonished and alarmed his friends. He poured out his energy to the last ounce. At one time we see him seated, exhausted, on the curbing of Jacob's well; at another time we see him falling asleep as soon as his head touched the pillow on the little boat which was carrying him back to Capernaum. When on the last day of his life they laid a beam of timber upon his shoulder he staggered under it and then fell, so completely had he been exhausted by the arduous labors of the preceding months and years. He saved others but himself he did not know how to save. He had thought and he gave it. He had ideas and he scattered them. He had truth and he shared it with men. Behold a sower goes forth to sow! It is Jesus. Look at him. Watch the swing of that arm. What a generous arm! He scatters the seed upon the beaten path. No matter. He scatters the seed on the soil that is rocky. What of it? He scatters the seed in brier patches and thorny corners. He does not mind that. The seed is abundant, and he will scatter it with a prodigal hand, hoping that some of it will find the soil which is fertile and which will bring forth a harvest to make glad the heart of God. Many a teacher has saved his best ideas for a chosen few. Jesus scattered his broadcast. He had often ignorant and prejudiced and unresponsive hearers, but he threw his pearls by the handful wherever he went. What glorious ideas he scattered over the crowds of Galilean farmers, what heavenly truths he unfolded to men and women of whom the world took no notice!

Never was a teacher such a spendthrift in the squandering of ideas, never did a great thinker pour out his treasures in such wild and immeasurable profusion. Freely he had received, and therefore freely he gave. It was not merely the work of the intellect, but also the blood of the heart which he gave. His affection toward men flowed in a stream constant and full. His sympathy covered all classes, and no individual, however low and despised, ever appealed to him in vain. Blind men on hearing of his approach lined themselves along the road crying as he passed, "Have mercy also on us." Lepers who were counted unclean and treated worse than dogs ventured to push their way into his presence and ask for a healing touch. Samaritans, the very offscourings of the world in the estimation of the orthodox Jew, knew that in this new rabbi they had a benefactor and friend. When he drove the traders out of the Temple it was the blind and the lame who came to him, knowing that they would not be cast away. Sympathy eats up the blood of the nerves, and he who sympathizes draws heavily on the fountains of energy. This Jesus always did. He was a man with a loving heart. He loved both his friends and his enemies. He loved them at the beginning and he loved them to the end. The love which he lavished upon his disciples purified them and bound them to him with bonds which nothing could break. But his love went out also to those who hated him and schemed to bring about his death. "Father, forgive them, for they know not what they do," it is in such a prayer that the loving heart of Jesus is clearly revealed. He poured out his love with a generosity which reminded men of the generosity of God. Having given time and strength and thought and sympathy and love, he finally gave up his life. More than this can no man give. He was not an unwilling victim of circumstances, or the helpless prey of ungovernable political forces, or a martyr like Caesar, or William the Silent, or Lincoln. He gave his life consciously and deliberately. It was not snatched from him by accident or fate, but freely surrendered by a heart willing to pay the great price. Again and again he endeavored to make this plain. "I have power to lay down my life," he said, "and I have power to take it again." It was his conviction from the beginning that he came into the world to minister to men's needs, and to give his life a ransom for many. It was only by the giving of his life that he could soften men's hearts and bring a lost world back to the Father's house.

This, then, was the earthly career of Jesus — one continuous manifestation of generous and boundless love. In his character we see not only what is possible for man to be, but we also behold a revelation of the character of the Eternal. "He that hath seen me hath seen the Father," so said Jesus to those who were the nearest to him, and it is a saying which should be often in our thoughts. In studying the character of Jesus we get light not only upon the possibilities of man, but also upon the disposition and the will of God. The God revealed by Jesus is the same God revealed by Nature. The God of Nature has always been known as a generous God. The days and nights, the sky and sea and land, the changing seasons, all bear witness to His amazing generosity. He is prodigal in all His doings. He is lavish in all His benefactions. He scatters good things with the bountiful munificence of a King. He scatters the stars not in paltry thousands but in countless millions. He creates flowers not in numbers which we can count, but in a profusion which confuses and confounds the imagination. He always gives more than can be accepted. He throws sunsets away on eyes which do not care for them. He gives fruit trees more blossoms than the trees can use. At every feast which He spreads there are fragments remaining filling twelve baskets. He is a munificent, free-handed, bountiful, and extravagant God.

He runs constantly to profusion and exuberance and overflowing plenty. He fills the measure, presses it down, shakes it together, and causes it to run over. The measure is full of beauty apparently going to waste. He breaks the alabaster box upon our head every day we live. He spreads a table before us. He makes our cup run over. There are a thousand toothsome things to eat, and a thousand lovely things to see, and a thousand exquisite pleasures to experience, and a thousand sublime truths to learn, and a thousand good opportunities to seize — more than we can ever make use of in the short span of life allowed us. In the realm of nature He is assuredly a lavish and bewilderingly bounteous God, and what He is in the world of nature He is likewise in the realm of the spirit. Jesus says, "Ask and ye shall receive." Do not hesitate to do it. No matter who you are, you may do it. "For every one that asketh, receiveth." It is an eternal principle, deep-seated in creation and deep-rooted in the heart of God, that gifts rich and royal may be had for the asking. It is the purpose of the Christian religion to bring us to a God who is willing to give us above what we are willing to ask or able to think. The generosity of Jesus is intended to remind us of the measureless beneficence of the all-Father. His message thrills with the thought that we constantly get not what we earn or what we deserve, but what an ungrudging and open-handed God is delighted to give.

If you ask why was Jesus generous, the answer is, God is love. When was love anything but liberal? When has love ever dealt out good things with a scant and skimping and miserly hand? When Peter suggested a certain number as being enough to indicate the limits of forgiveness, Jesus told him not to count at all. Love never counts. When did a mother ever count the number of times she kissed her baby, and when did a friend ever catalogue the number of favors toward his friend, or when did a parent ever make a list of all the good things he gave his children? Love never counts. It is the nature of love to give, and to keep on giving, and then to devise new ways of larger giving, and to imagine still additional needs which may be supplied. Speaking to fathers, Jesus says: "What man is there of you, who, if his son shall ask him for a loaf, will give him a stone; or if he shall ask for a fish, will he give him a serpent? If ye then being evil know how to give good gifts unto your children, how much more shall your Father which is in heaven give good things to them that ask him?" If you are ever tempted to question the generosity of the heart of God, look at Jesus! Once in the world's history there has lived a man whose supreme joy was ungrudging giving. He knew as no other man has ever known how much more blessed it is to give than to receive. He lived not to be ministered unto, but to minister; not to receive, but to give; not to save his life, but to pour it out for others. If generosity so great has appeared in Time, it must be because there is a generous heart in Eternity; if a grace so beautiful has blossomed on our earth, we have a right to expect the same grace in heaven.

"There's a wideness in God's mercy,
Like the wideness of the sea:
There's a kindness in his justice,
Which is more than liberty.
There is welcome for the sinner,
And more graces for the good;
There is mercy with the Saviour;
There is healing in his blood.
"For the love of God is broader

Than the measure of man's mind;
And the heart of the Eternal
Is most wonderfully kind.
If our love were but more simple,
We should take him at his word;
And our lives would be all sunshine
In the sweetness of our Lord."

XVII: THE CANDOR OF JESUS

"If it were not so I would have told you."
— John xiv: 2.

The word "candor" has a modern sense. In earlier times it meant whiteness or brightness, coming as it does from the old Latin word candidus, meaning "white," the word from which we get our word "candidate," signifying a man dressed in white, because aspirants for office in ancient Rome always dressed in white togas. But in modern speech candor is openness, fairness, outspokenness, sincerity. It is a rare virtue, one of the most winsome of all the virtues. Many a man does not possess it. He is taciturn, reserved, secretive. He keeps the door of his heart shut. When he says a thing you cannot tell how much he means, for you do not know the extent of his reservations. When he does a thing you cannot tell what he is going to do next, because you do not know how fully his act has embodied all which exists in his heart. He gives himself fully to no one. He is the man with the barred lips and the bolted heart. Such a man may be respected and even admired, but he cannot be loved. Jesus was loved. Men loved him so intensely they were willing to die for him. One reason was that he was a man with his heart open.

One obtains a hint of a man's disposition by noting the men whom he admires and praises. The trait which one sincerely likes to see in others is likely to be a feature of his own character. John in his Gospel tells us of a eulogy which Jesus passed one day upon a man named Nathaniel. Nathaniel was a citizen of a small Galilean village, Cana, situated not far from Nazareth. As soon as Philip had gotten a little acquainted with Jesus he was desirous of bringing Jesus and his friend Nathaniel together. Seeking Nathaniel he said enthusiastically, "We have found him!" to which came back the frigid answer, "Can there any good thing come out of Nazareth?" The two villages, Cana and Nazareth, were close together, and as frequently happens neither village saw much good in its neighbor. Great cities have been known to be bitterly jealous of one another, and this rivalry is sometimes more intense in the lives of competing towns. Nathaniel had a deep-seated contempt for dingy little Nazareth, and all that was in his heart came out in the cynical question, "Can there come any good thing out of Nazareth?" He was nothing if not frank. His friend, not at all daunted, mildly said, "Come and see." Whereupon the cynic immediately obeyed. He had his presuppositions, but he would not be enslaved by them. He had his prejudices, but he would not be held back by them. It was only reasonable that he should act on his friend's suggestion, and this he forthwith did. He was willing to investigate for himself. He had an open mind, an ingenuous heart. Jesus had been struck by his frank and noble face not long before when he had seen him praying under a fig tree. As soon as Jesus sees him coming toward him he exclaims in a tone musical with praise, "Behold an Israelite indeed in whom is no guile." This was the sort of man which won at once the heart of Jesus. There was no craft nor cunning in him, no duplicity nor deceit; he was a man of frank sincerity, and Jesus' heart immediately goes out to him, assuring him that over his open soul there is going to be an open heaven. Outspoken and frank himself, Jesus was en rapport with souls which were free from guile. And here we find one of the reasons why Jesus always extolled the disposition of a child. Without the child heart no man can enter heaven. And why? Because the child heart is always the open heart. Where can you find such candor, such beautiful frankness, such surprising and sometimes discomfiting outspokenness as in a little child? He will tell you just what he thinks, all he thinks, nothing will he hold back. He will make known his feelings, all his feelings, and will melt and overcome your heart by the fulness of his naive self-revelation. One of the reasons why Jesus set a child in the midst of the disciples, saying, "This is what you ought to be," is because a little child is the embodiment and personification of candor.

A man reveals himself in his dislikes as truly as in his prepossessions and praises. Whom did Jesus most dislike? The Pharisees. They were hypocrites. A hypocrite was an actor, a man who wore a mask, the mask representing a personality other than the one inside of it. "Do not be like the actors," this was his constant exhortation, and he never lost an opportunity of holding up the hypocrites to contempt and scorn. On one occasion he faced them in Jerusalem, calling them to their face "vipers." It was a harsh word, and yet it expressed the inmost spirit of the men to whom it was applied. They were as venomous and deadly as vipers. It is an awful thing to tarnish the name of God and render religion odious, and to poison the heart of the world. And yet all this these hypocrites were doing, and to the guileless heart of Jesus there were no men so repulsive and deserving of scorching condemnation. He was himself so genuine and open-hearted that the craft of these treacherous actors stirred him to blazing indignation.

He never held back the truth when it was time that the truth should be spoken. His loving heart told him when the hour had come. At the marriage feast in Cana he said to his mother who had come with imploring eyes and pleading tongue asking him to help the host out of the distressing predicament in which he found himself, "Woman, what have I to do with thee?" It had been predicted long before that a sword was to pass through Mary's heart, and here is surely one of the times when the sword passed through. The time has come when the mother's wishes can no longer be allowed to control the actions of the son. Her importunate requests can no longer determine the course of Jesus' action. The old days in Nazareth are forever gone, and a new epoch in Jesus' life has dawned, and in this larger realm the mother is nothing but a woman whose thoughts and feelings and wishes must be subordinated to the will of the man whom she has thus far called her son. What pain Jesus suffered in speaking thus we can only imagine. But he was the man with the open heart, and the wounding word had to be spoken.

The Gospels teem with illustrations of this surprising and daring frankness. One day in talking with some Sadducees — representatives of the aristocratic and influential classes of Palestine — he told them bluntly that they were always falling into error because they were so ignorant. They were ignorant both of the Scriptures and of the power of God. It was a needed word, for people who know little and think they know much are sometimes helped by having their attention called to the limitations of their knowledge; but to give such reprimand is not an easy thing to do. It was by his outspokenness that Jesus attempted to cure some of the infirmities of men.

His love of fairness comes out clearly in his warnings both to the twelve and to all who wanted to be numbered among his followers. He will hold back nothing. The whole terrible truth must be told. No man shall ever follow him without first knowing what risks and dangers discipleship involves. Read the tenth chapter of Matthew as a shining illustration of his candor. He wants the twelve to do his work, but before they start they shall know what sort of experiences they may reasonably expect. "Behold I send you forth as sheep in the midst of wolves," a figure which meant much to the men addressed who knew both sheep and wolves. Beginning thus he goes on to paint a picture black enough to daunt the heart of the bravest, and the only encouragement he has to give them for facing such awful dangers is the promise that he will confess them at last before his Father in heaven. No disciple shall ever say to him, "I did not know what it meant!" or shall ever chide him with the question, "Why did you not tell me?" When men came rushing to him saying, "Master, I will follow you," he flashed on them the gloom of a dark sentence, unwilling to accept the allegiance of any one, even in times when he most needed support, without having first revealed to the volunteer the full significance of a place in his ranks. Men's heads were filled with dreams of supremacy and sovereignty and glory, and more than one heart was chilled by the searching question, "Are you able to drink the cup?" His candor reduced the number of his followers, but it was just like him to hold back nothing which men had a right to know.

But it is in his confessions that his candor reaches its climax. Among his confessions there are three which must here have our attention. He admits without hesitation that there was a limitation of his authority. One day a man interrupted him with the cry, "Speak to my brother that he divide the inheritance with me," and the reply was, "Man, who made me a judge or a divider over you?" There was a realm then in which Jesus was not ordained to act. This was a surprising confession for the Messiah to make. It had been the dream of the prophets that the Messiah should have authority over all the kingdoms of life, that every form of injustice should be trampled under his feet. The nation had long pictured a king who should put an end to the cruel inequalities with which the world was cursed, and measure out justice with an even hand. And now the Messiah deliberately turns his back on a man who is pleading for justice, saying that into that realm he cannot now enter. Only a strong man is brave enough to disappoint his friends by candidly admitting that it is impossible for him to do what they have expected of him. Not only did Jesus confess a limitation of his authority, but also of his power. When two of his disciples asked for the chief places in the new kingdom, he frankly told them that he did not have the power to select his own prime ministers, because all such matters were hidden in the deep counsels of God.

More surprising was his confession of ignorance. An ignorant Messiah was to the pious and instructed Hebrew an impossible conception. The Messiah was not only to be able to do everything, he was also to know everything. The tradition was firmly lodged in the hearts of the Samaritans as well as of the Jews, as we see in the words of the woman of Samaria, "I know that Messiah cometh: when he is come he will tell us all things." But Jesus frankly admitted that there were things which he did not know. For instance, one day he was talking in graphic phrase about the end of the world. He spoke of it so definitely and positively that it was a natural inference that he knew just when it would take place. To the amazement of his hearers he said, "Of that day and that hour knoweth no man, no, not the angels which are in heaven, neither the Son, but the Father." There is nothing which so weakens the authority of a teacher with the public as the discovery of his ignorance in regard to a matter on which it is generally considered his business to be informed. There is no confession which a teacher makes so reluctantly and with such hazards as that of ignorance on a point which lies within his province. It shatters popular confidence, and robs his words of authority, and cripples all his subsequent work. Candid, indeed, is the teacher who confesses his ignorance. Jesus confessed his. He knew the risks and he took them. He knew his words could be misconstrued and that they would become to thousands a stumbling-block, but he spoke them.

Again and yet again his friends and followers, less candid than their Master, have shrunk back from his bold confession and have watered down his words, trying to make them mean less than they carry on their face. Many a tricky interpretation has been given to his declaration by those who have not been willing to think of Jesus as being anything but omniscient, and have feared that men if once told of one deficiency in Jesus' knowledge might hesitate to give him the fulness of their trust and refuse to bow before him as King of kings and Lord of lords. But men who thus try to evade the plain language of Scripture are not candid. Let us be thankful that Peter was frank enough to tell Mark just what Jesus said, and that Mark was sincere enough to write down just what Peter reported, and that Matthew in a book written especially to prove that Jesus was the long-expected Messiah and King of Israel, did not shrink from writing down the great confession of Jesus' ignorance as to the day and the hour of the end of the world. The New Testament is like its hero, gloriously candid. It points to Jesus saying, "This is the Messiah, the Son of God," and then it tells us that men spat upon him.

Nothing inspires confidence in a man like candor. If a man is frank and open in nine points, we may safely trust him in the tenth. Jesus makes his candor a reason why his disciples ought to trust him in those realms of thought and life which lie beyond their sight. "In my Father's house are many mansions, if it were not so I would have told you." Of course he would. It was his nature to tell men everything it was necessary for them to know. He would not allow his friends to go on holding delusions when a word from him would set them free. These men had in them an instinctive belief in the life to come. Like all normal and unspoiled men they believed that death is not the end. They looked forward to a life of larger scope and rapture than any which this world can know. Jesus allowed them to nourish these expectations. He saw the direction in which their faces all were set, and he did not tell them they were swayed by an illusion. He let them go on thinking of heaven, hoping for heaven, working for heaven, and now that the end of his earthly life has come, he tells them more plainly of the nature of this vast world just beyond the shadow.

Carry this thought with you in your reading of the New Testament, and it will give you fresh confidence in many things which we believe about Jesus. We believe that he was sinless. Why? Because of a sentence here and there like, "Which one of you convinceth me of sin?" That foundation might prove somewhat precarious. Shall we think he was sinless because he never committed a sinful act? But how do you know, how can you know, about his thoughts and feelings and motives, and what proof have you that his motives and feelings and thoughts were always altogether just what God would have them to be? The best reason we have for believing in the sinlessness of Jesus is the fact that he allowed his dearest friends to think that he was. There is in all his talk no trace of regret or hint of compunction, or suggestion of sorrow for shortcoming or slightest vestige of remorse. He taught other men to think of themselves as sinners, he asserted plainly that the human heart is evil, he told his disciples that every time they prayed they were to pray to be forgiven, but he never speaks or acts as though he himself has the faintest consciousness of having ever done anything other than what was pleasing to God. This is remarkable, unparalleled. All the saints beat their breasts saying, "God be merciful to me a sinner." The purer the heart the lower it bows before infinite holiness. Jesus never by word or by act indicates that he is conscious of falling short of the wishes of God. If he had been, would he not have said so? His was the open heart. Would he deceive men on a matter of such cardinal moment? Is this like him to be conscious of transgression, and conscience-stricken because of his sins and never indicate by a word that he like the disciples must pray to be forgiven? They thought he was sinless. Would this man with the open heart and the open mouth allow his dearest friends to be deceived? He was without sin even as the apostle said he was. We are sure of it for the reason that if he had not been he would have told us.

On his candor, then, we have a right to build both for time and eternity. When he says that if we do not repent we shall perish, and that only those who are born from above enter the kingdom of light, we have every reason for believing that these statements are true. And when he says that his disciples are going to do greater things than were ever done in Palestine, and that he will be with us always even unto the end of the world, why should we not believe him?

And since he is so frank and open with us why should not we be open-hearted and frank with him? If he tells us truly the things in his heart, why should we not tell him truly the things which are in our hearts? He has given himself to us: why do we not give ourselves to him?

XVIII: THE ENTHUSIASM OF JESUS

"I came to cast fire upon the earth."
— Luke xii: 49.

Strange to say, the word "enthusiasm" does not occur in our English New Testament, nor is it to be found in the Greek Testament; and yet the New Testament is the most enthusiastic of all books, and Jesus is the most enthusiastic of all men. The word "enthusiasm" is avoided, and for a reason. In the first century it had unsavory associations. Enthusiasm in the Pagan world was an ecstasy, or divine possession. An enthusiast was one who was inspired or possessed by a god. Often the enthusiast was a fanatic, sometimes he was a madman. The evangelists and apostles did not like the word, and so they kept it out of their writings. In the speech of to-day, enthusiasm is a noble word. It is fervor of mind, ardency of spirit, exaltation of soul. It is passion, heat, fire. Though the word is absent, the thing itself is present. Jesus burns with fervent heat. His very words are sparks which kindle conflagrations.

When a boy he visited Jerusalem with his parents, and slipping one day into the Temple to hear the scholars discussing the great problems of religion, he lost himself. He forgot what day of the week it was, and what hour of the day it was. His father and mother and brothers and sisters and friends all passed completely from his mind. He plunged headlong into the discussion of the doctors, gave himself up completely to the subject of the hour, allowed himself to be swept along on the tide of thought and discussion, until all at once his mother's face appeared at the door and he was reminded of the place he had left vacant in the caravan which had started toward Galilee. In this temple experience we see a nature sensitive and impressionable, capable of being heated to high temperatures.

When as a young man of thirty he next appears before us we see him at the river Jordan being baptized by the mighty preacher John. Immediately after the baptism, St. Mark tells us he was "driven" by the Spirit into the wilderness. The word "driven" has in it a significance which is revealing. Jesus is so full of feeling after the experience which came to him in his baptism that he cannot linger near the homes of men, but must at once rush away into unfrequented and desert places where he can meditate upon the strange thing that has happened to him, and ponder the steps which he must next take. From this time on we have a man before us who is being driven. Even when a boy he used a word which expressed the intensity of his feeling, "Do you not know that I must be about my Father's business?" He never ceased to use that word "must." They wanted him to stay in Capernaum, but he could not do it. "I must preach the gospel of the kingdom of God to the other cities also." They wanted him to stay away from Jerusalem, knowing that it was dangerous there, but he said: "I must go to Jerusalem. I have a baptism to be baptized with, and how am I straitened until it be accomplished?" He felt that his life would be short and so he kept saying, "I must work the works of Him that sent me while it is day: the night cometh when no man can work."

How intense his life was we can see in what is told us of his habit of praying. He was always praying. He arose early in the morning in order to find more time to pray, he stayed up late at night in order to increase the hours in which he might speak to God. Sometimes he did not go to bed at all, remaining all night long upon some hilltop under the stars pouring out his soul to God. He was enthusiastic in prayer, and therefore he was zealous in work. Men were astounded by the magnitude of his labors. Sometimes he did not take time to eat. Even when he went away for a season of relaxation he gave himself up to the crowds which pursued him. His words have in them an energy which burns. Again and again we catch expressions in which we can feel his great heart beating: "I have not found so great faith, no, not in Israel," "O woman, great is thy faith!" "I thank thee, O Father!" "O Jerusalem, Jerusalem, how often!" All these are out of the throat of an enthusiast, a man surcharged with feeling. At the distance of nineteen hundred years from the day on which they were spoken our heart leaps when we listen to them. The rains of the centuries have not put out their fire.

But it is not simply what Jesus says, but also what those who touched him say which lets us look into the molten centre of his glowing heart. Mark frankly tells us that there was a time in Jesus' life when his labor was so excessive that his friends said, "He is beside himself." Expressive, indeed, is the phrase. A man is beside himself when he is a little "off." He is not "away off," for then he is out of his head, or insane. But when a man has swung just a little from his balance he is beside himself. He is in the borderland which is between sanity and insanity. Such burning earnestness in the work of doing good had never been seen in Palestine. No wonder men said, "He is beside himself!" But this was the judgment of his friends. His enemies did not hesitate to say boldly, "He has a devil, he is mad." Jesus made this impression not once, but often. Such zeal for righteousness, such enthusiasm for helping men seemed to the cold-blooded scribes the fury of a maniac. It was when Paul was burning with the same kind of heat that Festus cried, "Paul, thou art mad!" Nothing seems so crazy as enthusiasm to a man incapable of feeling it.

The crowds also bear witness to the fire which this man had in him. He stirred men up wherever he went. They crowded him off the land upon the water. They pushed him off the plain up the hillside. They crowded the houses in which he tarried, they pressed round him as he walked through the streets. Again and again the excitement rose to fever heat, and Jesus slipped away and hid himself. Near the close of his career the crowds went wild in their tumultuous joy, shouting, singing, casting their clothing in the dust that the animal which Jesus rode might have a carpet for its hoofs like unto that furnished for triumphal processions of kings. No man can set a crowd blazing unless his own soul is ablaze. When we see some men hurrahing and adoring and other men gnashing their teeth and cursing, some boiling with love, others seething with hate, it is evident we are in the presence of a man whose heart glows like a furnace and whose soul radiates heat wherever he goes.

A still finer evidence of this is found in the character of the men whom Jesus attracted to him as his intimate friends. The apostles were all men of fire. Do not believe the pictures when they paint the twelve as limp and pallid men. They were full-blooded, virile, mighty men, full of fire and passion, drawn to Jesus because in him they saw a man who satisfied them. Peter had a seething soul, his words roll out of him like molten lava. John and James were called Sons of Thunder. The disciple whom Jesus loved was so passionate that he wanted to burn up a whole town which had insulted his Master. One of the disciples was a zealot, a member of the most radical political party in Palestine. Men of this party could scarcely sleep, so intense was their hatred of Rome, and no man among the zealots could ever have been attracted by a cold-blooded, limp-handed man. It was because Jesus had in him the fire which the zealots loved that Simon enrolled himself among the apostles. Judas also was a man made of inflammable stuff. His remorse sets him on fire and there is nothing more thrilling in history than his shriek: "I have sinned! I have sinned!" If there was a lethargic temperament in the apostolic company, it was that of Thomas; but even he was so devoted to Jesus that at a crisis in his life he said to his comrades, "Come, let us go and die with him." That was the feeling of them all. They loved Jesus with such an intensity of devotion, such a passionate self-abandon, that they were ready at any moment to lay down their lives for him. No man can win and hold the ardent devotion of strong men unless he has a soul which is hot. Jesus from first to last was surrounded by enthusiasts because he himself was enthusiastic.

If you ask for the cause of this enthusiasm, you will find that it has three roots. In the first place, Jesus had a sensitive nature. He was finely organized, his nerves were delicately strung. There is a vast difference in the make-up of men. Some men are coarse, stolid, heavy. They have sensations but not intense ones. They have the emotions of vegetables. There are other men who are as delicately adjusted as an asolian harp. Every breeze that blows over them causes them to vibrate and wooes from them music. Such a man was Jesus. No finer clay was ever organized around a soul than that which formed his body, and this body was never coarsened or calloused by sin. On the Mount of Transfiguration his soul so shone through his body that his disciples were awed and overwhelmed. In the Garden of Gethsemane his agony was so great that the perspiration on his brow looked in the moonlight like huge drops of blood. When his soul at one time came into his face men fell backward to the ground.

Along with this nature capable of burning there existed a vision of God and a vision of man which set the nation on fire. Jesus saw that the maker of the universe is a Father, that at the centre of things there beats a Father's heart, that over all there extends a Father's care, and that to all there flows a Father's love. Other men have seen this dimly, as it were through a glass darkly, but Jesus saw it as it had never been seen before and as it has never been seen since. It was to him the one clear and luminous fact of the universe and everything else was seen in the glory of this stupendous truth. Since God is the all-Father, then all men are His children. He created them all, He loves them all. He desires to save them all. No matter who they are or what they are or where they are, they are His children, and they cannot drift beyond His love and care. Men everywhere are brothers, and for one brother to help another, this is the supreme joy in living. Other men see this dimly, but to Jesus it was all clear as the sun at noon. With such a vision of God and such a vision of man is it to be wondered at that his soul burned like a star? Out of such a nature heated hot by such a vision there came forth a purpose, steadfast and full of passion. To the clear eye of Jesus a mighty battle was raging on the earth. There was a terrific conflict between right and wrong, light and darkness, good and evil, God and the Devil. There was nothing to do at such a crisis but to throw himself whole-heartedly into the contest, fighting indomitably for the glory of the Father and the welfare of his brethren. Put these three things together — a sensitive and inflammable nature, a clear and glorious vision, and a fiery and indomitable purpose — and you have the ingredients which go to produce the divine flame which is known as enthusiasm.

What a beautiful thing it is, enthusiasm! Moses turned aside to see a burning bush, everybody turns aside to see a burning man. Glance across the centuries and you will note that every time the race has turned aside from the beaten path it has been to see a man who was burning. Enthusiasm is of different kinds, but every kind is fascinating. There is what we may call physical enthusiasm, the enthusiasm of the nerves and the blood. It is this enthusiasm which was kindled at the great athletic contests in Greece, and which blazes at our modern football contests. To be one of forty thousand people watching a few strong men engaged in a strenuous game stirs the nerves and sets the corpuscles in the blood to hurrahing. It is not a high form of enthusiasm, but it is glorious, and men will go miles to experience the thrill. Much higher than this is intellectual enthusiasm, the fervor which men feel in the pursuit of truth. This is the enthusiasm of explorers and discoverers and inventors and scholars — men who devote their lives to the sublime work of snatching a new kingdom from the clutch of the unknown. Men count not their lives dear in the pursuit of knowledge. When we read of an explorer dying in a wild and desert land, or of a physician giving up his life in the laboratory in search of a secret which will diminish pain or lengthen life, we are awed into silence. The heart knows that it stands in the presence of something divine. Above this is the aesthetic enthusiasm, fiery zeal in the pursuit of beauty. There are men and women in whose eyes there is a hunger after beauty which we who do not have it cannot understand. The man with the artistic eye is seeking everywhere for beauty. When his eyelids fall, his soul still sees forms, colors, lights, shadows, scenes of loveliness and perfection. What a history it is, the history of art. What a line of heroes and martyrs have travelled the steep and thorny road.

Many a man has painted day by day until his eyes began to fail, and then he has painted on and on amid the deepening shadows, never faltering, never surrendering until the final darkness falls. Others have in their ears a hunger after harmony. All through life they thirst for fuller measures of lovely tones. There is no temple for them but the vast and glorious temple of music, and melodies and divine sequences of ordered tones flow in a constant tide through the soul. What biographies they are, the biographies of musicians. For many of them it has been a life of labor, privation, sacrifice, disappointment, poverty; but all things precious have been counted dross by souls in pursuit of higher strains of the heavenly anthem. Before all such martyrs the soul takes off its shoes, knowing that the ground is holy. But higher than all enthusiasms is the fire that burns in souls in love with God. To know Him, to serve Him, to glorify Him, this is the highest ambition of which the soul is capable, and the soul when possessed with this ambition burns with a fire that cannot be quenched. This was the enthusiasm of Jesus. In him the highest of the enthusiasms reached its climax. He lived and moved and had his being in the presence of the Eternal. From the beginning to the end he saw the majesty of righteousness, loved the beauty of holiness, and lived for the glory of God.

It is not to be wondered at, then, that the religion of Jesus likes the word "fire." John the Baptist declared that he could baptize only with water but that one was coming who would baptize with fire. From John's hands men came dripping, from Jesus' hands they came blazing. St. Luke tells us that on the Day of Pentecost there seemed to be a flame on every forehead, fit emblem of the new religion's heart. John on the isle of Patmos thinking of Jesus sees him with eyes like flames of fire and feet of burnished brass. He hears him talking to the Laodiceans, and this is what he says: "I would thou wert cold or hot. Because thou art lukewarm, and neither hot nor cold, I will spew you out of my mouth." One can drink cold water with a relish. He can also drink water heated to a certain temperature. But against tepid water the stomach rebels. The beloved disciple does not hesitate to represent Jesus saying, "Lukewarm Christians are nauseating to me!"

And alas! how many lukewarm Christians there are, men who are indifferent, neutral, neither hot nor cold. They do not oppose, they approve, but approbation cannot set the world on fire. Approbation is a nod of one corner of the intellect, enthusiasm is the smile of the soul. What is the matter with Christians that they are so lacking in enthusiasm? The answer is that the nature is saturated, soaked by the chilling drizzle of worldliness, and along with this deterioration of nature comes a diminishing of the vision of the Fatherhood of God and the Brotherhood of man, and because there is a shadowed vision the glowing purpose is also lacking, and the soul does not catch fire. What, then, shall we do? Let us go back to Him who is a zealous God, so eager and ardent in His love that He gave His only begotten Son. If we are not ablaze in the presence of such a gospel, it is because we have a heart of stone; but He who knows our frame and who remembers that we are dust has promised to remove the heart of stone and to give us a heart of flesh.

XIX: THE GLADNESS OF JESUS

"Rejoice, and be exceeding glad."
— Matthew v: 12.

We are trying to see Jesus of Nazareth! Our one question is: What kind of man was he? We are not studying his personality or considering his ideas — all we want to know is what kind of a man he was, how did he impress the people who saw him in Galilee and Judea. We are trying to get rid of impressions which have been made upon us by painters and our own imagination. It is by no means easy to see him as he was, the mists blow in between us and him, and blur the features of his face. The dust settles upon the picture which the evangelists have painted and the man becomes dim to our eyes. All sorts of men — poets, philosophers, painters — have like so many human spiders woven cobwebs over the picture, so that until we brush the cobwebs away it is impossible to see him. In the words of the familiar hymn, "We would see Jesus," we would bring him out of the shadows and see him as he is. It is an interesting enterprise in which we are engaged, because all the Christian churches take their name from this man. The churches differ widely from one another in worship, in government, in teachings, — Protestants of many kinds are separated from one another, and Catholics of many classes are also separated from one another, — but this one thing is remarkable, that all the Christian churches of the world are clinging tenaciously to the garments of this man. They all without exception call him Master; they all hold him up as the pattern of a perfect life. "He," they say, "is our example. We are to reproduce the characteristic notes displayed in him." And therefore it becomes not only an interesting enterprise, but one of tremendous importance, this effort to find out what kind of man he was. If we get a distorted image of him, we harm ourselves and rob the world. Just in proportion as we see him clearly and understand precisely what sort of man he was, do we become able to pattern our lives after his and become the men God would have us to be.

Pushing then all the poets and philosophers aside, let us ask ourselves the question: Did Jesus of Nazareth impress men as glad or sad, solemn or radiant, jubilant or melancholy? There is no doubt about the answer which the painters give. They nearly always paint him sad, they love to paint him on the cross, they picture him dying with a great melancholy in his eyes — or if they do not paint him on the cross, they paint him on the way to the cross with the crown of thorns on his head, bending under the burden as he staggers up Golgotha. In all the Catholic churches of the world you see the twelve stations of the cross. The Jesus of Christian history is a man of sorrows and acquainted with grief; there is sadness in his face and a great pang in his heart. Christianity is the religion of sorrow, said Goethe, and Carlyle declared that Goethe's judgment was correct. And not only do the painters paint him sad, but so also does our imagination. When we think of him we think of him as crucified. In that wonderful painting of Hoi man Hunt the cross on which Jesus died casts a shadow out across Jerusalem to the end of the world, and that is what the cross does in the pictures which our mind paints of Jesus and the world in which he lived — we always see him with the shadow of the cross upon him, we always think of him as severe and sad. But we cannot afford to follow the painters. They paint Jesus with a halo. Nobody in Jerusalem ever saw the halo. They paint him with a shadow on his face — do you suppose the men in Palestine saw the shadow? We want to see him as he was.

In order to find out what impression he really made upon the people of his day, it will be worth our while to listen to what his enemies had to say. Of course his enemies will not speak the ungarbled truth, they will deal in falsehoods; but even falsehoods are of great advantage in trying to make one's way toward the truth. There is nothing that so dumfounds a lawyer in the questioning of a witness as unbroken silence. If a witness will only speak, if he will only speak falsehoods, his speech is more illuminating than continuous silence, for falsehoods when arranged in a row have a curious fashion of pointing in the direction of the truth. When a man begins lying, if you can only keep him lying long enough, he will by and by put you on the track of discovering what the truth is. And so it is with the enemies of Jesus. They have said certain things which are invaluable to us in our search after authentic knowledge of the character of Jesus. Among other things which they said, they declared he was a glutton. Of course he was not, but they said he was. Now a glutton is never a glum and sourfaced man. Gluttony is a form of pleasure. Men overeat because overeating gives enjoyment. A glutton is likely to be round and rotund. When the men of Jesus' day said he was a glutton we may rest assured he was not an ascetic in his looks or habits. They also called him a wine bibber. Of course he was not, but the very fact that they accused him of guzzling wine points in the direction of the kind of man he was. A wine bibber is usually a jolly man. Wine unlocks the lips and gives temporary brilliancy to the mind. A man under the influence of wine is exceedingly social and talkative and genial. The enemies of Jesus would never have called him a wine bibber if he had been as glum and sad as some of the artists have painted him. They called him also the friend of publicans and sinners. By publicans and sinners we are to understand non-churchgoers. This man not only went to church and associated with pious people, but he associated with people who had no piety at all. When they declared he was a friend of these non-churchgoers, they implied that he was of the same stripe as they — "Birds of a feather always flock together." He would never have associated with such godless people if he himself had not had a godless heart. So his enemies declared, and if Jesus had been taciturn and sullen, grim and morose, his enemies would never have declared he was a boon companion of light-hearted men. Their lying would have taken another form. Put, then, these three bits of falsehood together, and what is the direction in which they point? They are the most precious bits of slander that ever slipped from slimy lips. They prove indisputably that whatever Jesus was or was not, he was not morose or sour or melancholy.

Having listened to the testimony of his enemies, let us now study one of the words Jesus applied to himself. There were pious people in Palestine who were greatly scandalized because Jesus never fasted, nor did he teach his disciples that it was their duty to fast. Fasting was a recognized feature of the Jewish religion. Every person of orthodox piety in Palestine fasted twice every week. Fasting had been prescribed by the greatest of the rabbis; it had also been the requirement of John the Baptist himself. Some people came to Jesus one day in disgust, saying, "Why do your disciples not fast?" The reply of Jesus is illuminating. He said, "How can the children of the bridechamber fast when the bridegroom is with them?" Did you ever mark the use of that word "bridegroom"? Jesus says that he is a bridegroom. He seized upon a word that is the symbol of human joy. If ever a man is happy in this world, it is on his wedding day. Jesus says that he lives in an atmosphere of wedding joy, and so also do his disciples. It is impossible therefore for either him or his disciples to take up any of the old fashions of the grim and solemn piety of the past. He told the men who criticised him that his life was different from the life of John the Baptist and also from the life of the Pharisees. You cannot mix the two kinds of piety, the two forms of life will not mingle. Let me give you an illustration or two, he said: "A man does not put a new patch on an old garment, because the new patch will tear out and the rent will be still worse. Neither can you put my form of life on to the old form of piety, the two will not hold together, the strength that is in my form of life will simply tear the old form of life to pieces. Or, to give you another illustration, men do not put new wine into old wine skins, for there is too much life and movement and sparkle in new wine for the old skins. If you attempt to put the new wine into the old skins, the old skins will burst and the wine will be lost. So do not think that you can put the new life which I live and which I want all my followers to live into old forms of pharisaic piety, for this cannot be done. I am living a new kind of life, and I want a new kind of man, a new spirit, a new form of religion."

It would seem, then, that Jesus was a man abounding in joy. Gladness was one of the notes of his character. Listen to him as he teaches, and again and again you catch the notes of happiness. He was all the time saying, "Unless you become like a little! child, you cannot enter the kingdom of God" — and; what was it in the little child that attracted him? One thing which attracted him was the child's sunny heart. What would we do in this world without the children laughing away the cares and sighs? Have you ever listened to their laughter in the streets while the funeral procession was passing by? Have you ever seen a golden-haired little child with beaming face at the centre of a room in which there was a casket around which broken-hearted men and women were gathering? Look at that child in the centre of the chamber of death — that is the picture of the Christian amid the shadows of this darkened world. Or listen again to what he says about worry. He defines it as one of the deadliest of all sins. We are not to worry about the present, about the necessities of existence, about to-morrow, about what we ought to do or say in the great crises which lie ahead of us. It is not right, he says; it is contrary to the law of God. Look at nature: see the lilies and the birds, there is not a trace of solicitude in all nature's lovely face. Listen again to the exhortations which he gives his disciples. He tells them that when men persecute them and say all manner of evil against them falsely, they are to rejoice and be exceeding glad. The English translation does not do justice to the Greek. He says, "Rejoice and leap for joy." Let your joy express itself. When matters are at their worst, then you ought to have the happiness which leaps. Certainly a sad-hearted man could never give advice like that. Listen to him again as he says to the great crowds, "Come unto me all ye that labor and are heavy laden, and I will give you rest; for my yoke is easy and my burden is light." A glum-faced prophet could never speak so. He was glad even to the end. Even in the upper chamber, with death only a few hours away, he goes right on speaking of the joy that is bubbling up in his own heart and he prays that the same joy may abound in the hearts of those that love him. He tells his disciples that all of his teaching has been granted unto them because of his desire that his joy might remain in them and that their joy might be full. There was no shadow on his face that night in the upper chamber. The cross is near, but it casts no shadow.

But does not the New Testament say that Jesus wept? It does. And does the New Testament ever say that Jesus laughed? It does not. Are we therefore to infer that Jesus often wept and never laughed? The inference is unfounded. Why does the New Testament say that Jesus wept? Probably because it was so exceptional. It is the exceptional thing that is written down. There are four million people in New York City, let one of them kill another — he gets at once into the papers. Murder is exceptional and so it is always noted. Thousands of people walk the streets, let one of them fall and break his leg and that accident is noted — no attention is paid to the thousands who meet with no accident. Jesus laughed so frequently it was not worth while calling attention to it. He wept so seldom that when he did weep it struck the disciples with consternation. John could never forget it. He remembered the day at the tomb of Lazarus when Mary was weeping and her sister and all the relatives and friends, and it was then that Jesus wept, so tender and sympathetic was he that he broke down — that great strong, radiant, exuberant man wept. John says that the world itself could not contain the books that could be written if he attempted to put down all the things which Jesus said and did. He will crowd back a million things, to make room for that one surprising fact that at the grave of Lazarus Jesus wept. The sentence instead of proving that Jesus was lachrymose and doleful bears eloquent witness to the fact that Jesus was buoyant and exultant.

A Christian must then, if he would follow Jesus, be a joyous and jubilant man. Some one says at once, "Ah, I know many Christians who are anything but happy, they are the most doleful creatures in all the world, they whine and whimper, they sob and cry, their very faces are images of woe — how will you explain that?" The explanation is that all such persons although they profess to follow Jesus, follow him afar off. You may be tempted to say that glum and dismal Christians are not Christians at all. That is probably somewhat too severe. It would be nearer right to say that they are not developed Christians, mature or ripened Christians. The very finest apples, you know, in the earlier stages of their growth are sour and green. It is not until the sun has done his perfect work that they are golden and luscious. Just so it is with souls in the earlier stages of development — they are often green and sour, crabbed, and full of acid. But if they will only subject themselves to the shining of the sun, the great joyous, exuberant, laughing sun, all the juices of their nature will grow sweet and mellow, and they will find themselves at last in the kingdom of peace and joy.

It is the tragedy of this world that there are so many people in it who find it impossible to rejoice. What is the matter with you that you are not happier than you are? Certainly there is something wrong! What a pity it is to live in a world like this and not enjoy living! It is amazing that any one should live in a universe so glorious, and not feel like shouting! If you are lachrymose and drooping it is because there is something wrong. You are not well in body or in mind, or it may be you are sick in both. You have not yet learned the high art of living, you have not yet come to Jesus. Why not come and sit at his feet? Why not take his yoke upon you and learn of him, for his yoke is easy and his burden is light.

XX: THE HUMILITY OF JESUS

"I am meek and lowly in heart."
— Matthew xi: 29.

Let us begin with that wonderful verse in the eleventh chapter of the Gospel according to St. Matthew: "Come unto me, all ye that labor and are heavy laden; and I will give you rest. Take my yoke upon you, and learn of me; for I am meek and lowly in heart: and ye shall find rest unto your souls." That sentence is unique in the Gospel. There is nothing else at all like it. It is a bit of autobiography which is immeasurably precious. Nowhere is Jesus recorded as having said, "Come unto me, for I am patient — for I am courageous — for I am self-sacrificing;" but here for the first time he calls attention to one of his characteristics. He has allowed other men to call attention to this virtue or that grace, but he himself will bring out the fact that he is humble. At this point he takes the brush in his own hand, saying, "I will put this color on myself." So unusual is the sentence that some men have been scandalized by it. They have declared he never said it, that it is not like him, that he could not say it, that if he did say it, it reveals a defect in his character. These men tell us that a man cannot eulogize himself, that it is always improper for a man to sing his own praises. All of which may be true, but this is a fair question: Is it right for a man ever to describe himself? Is it proper for a man to give a reason why men should come to him and take lessons of him? I think it is. That is all Jesus does in this instance. He says, "Come unto me, I have something to teach you, I should like to teach you humility."

Possibly no other virtue in the catalogue of Christian virtues is so misunderstood as this one. No other one has been so often erroneously defined, no other grace has been so persistently counterfeited and caricatured. What do we mean by humility? If you should have asked that question in the streets of ancient Athens, men would have told you that humility is something mean, it is cowardly, cringing, groveling; humility is meanness of spirit, it is something low and selfish, it is a characteristic of slaves. If a Greek had called another Greek humble, the Greek would have been insulted by the epithet. In all the Pagan world there was no virtue known as humility. Humility was always and everywhere a defect, a blemish, a vice.

But what do we mean by humility? The question is not so easily answered as it might seem. Humility is a Christian virtue — everybody says it is. We know that Jesus was humble, we know also that he demands humility of us, we know that he took the ancient word and cleansed it and made it a lovely word, and yet when asked to define the meaning of it, how difficult it is to do. What a variety of answers we have in answer to the question what humility is! One person says it is taking a low estimate of one's deserts; another says it is making one's self small. Another says it is a sense of inferiority in the presence of others. Another says it is a sense of imperfection, or of ill desert. Another says that it is softness, passivity, a willingness to submit. Now all of these definitions are proved to be erroneous the moment we carry them into the atmosphere of the New Testament. The humility which Jesus requires of those who follow him is the humility which he had himself, and certainly his humility was not meanness of spirit. There was nothing cringing or crawling in him. When has there walked the earth a man who held his head higher than did he? When has the world known a man of such lofty, regnant spirit? Nor did he take a low estimate of himself. On the other hand, no man ever estimated himself so highly. Hear him saying to the astounded crowd: "It was said to you by them of old time — but I say unto you," thus putting himself higher than Moses. Listen to him as he says: "A greater than Solomon is here," "I am the good shepherd," "I am the light of the world," "I am the way, the truth, and the life," "I am from above," "No man knows the Father but the Son," "No man comes to the Father save through me," "I, if I be lifted up, will draw all men unto me." Certainly humility on the lips of Jesus does not mean a low estimate of one's powers. Let us then come close to him in order to understand just what he means when he says, "I am meek and lowly in heart."

Jesus gave his disciples three great lessons on the subject of humility, and to these I invite your attention. You will find the first of them recorded in the eighteenth of Matthew, the first five verses. On a certain occasion Jesus takes a little child, and putting him in the midst, says: "Whoever shall humble himself as a little child the same shall be great in the kingdom of heaven. Except ye become as a little child, ye shall in no wise enter into the kingdom of heaven." The words have been repeated to us so frequently they fail to surprise the heart. This is one of the great scenes in the history of the world, one of the original scenes. Nothing like it was ever known in the history of Assyria, or of Babylonia, or of Egypt, or of Persia, or of Greece or Rome. It is unique, absolutely original. "Whosoever shall humble himself as a little child" — and what is the crowning characteristic of a little Child? It is teachableness, docility, willingness to learn. A child is eager for knowledge, he is everlastingly asking questions, he is always bent on investigation, he pries into everything. He wants to go to the roots of everything. He always wants you to tell him one more story, he will wear a half dozen grown people out simply by the questions which he asks — so hungry is he for knowledge. This teachableness is humility.

Not only is he free from self-sufficiency, but he is free from vanity. A little child is not vain of the belongings of its parents. It cares nothing for diamonds or silks, brown stone, or carriages. It plays with perfect contentment with a child in the street whose parents have no carriages and who are too poor to own diamonds. Free from vanity it also knows nothing of ambition, it knows nothing of social aspirations. Place before it the queen of England and its own mother, and it will choose its mother every time, though she be nothing but a washwoman — so simple, so human, so beautiful is the heart of a child. It is this characteristic of the child heart that Jesus loves. It was because the Pharisees did not have it that he criticised them and condemned them. They were not teachable, they knew everything. Nobody could tell them anything. They were vain, they blew trumpets and called attention to their decorations. They loved salutations. They were ambitious, they were always pushing themselves forward, taking the chief places at the feasts. He could do nothing with them because they were not humble. He, on the other hand, had the heart of a child. The evangelists do not tell us about the first twelve years of his life, but in imagination we can see him sitting at the feet of his mother drinking in knowledge from her lips. We can see him in the little school in Nazareth, studying, hungry for knowledge. We get just a glimpse of him at the age of twelve, so hungry for knowledge that he will not go home, but lingers behind to ask the big teachers in the Temple just one more question. Always was he teachable. There is no trace of arrogance in him, no spirit of assumption. He is constantly talking to God, asking him questions, praying for new light. He cannot live without prayer. Prayer is the language of humility. Only the docile in heart ever pray. When we say that Jesus was a man of prayer, we say he was meek and lowly in heart.

Let us now turn to the twentieth of Matthew, verses twenty-five to twenty-eight. His disciples, in spite of all his admonitions and teachings, are filled with the ambitious spirit. They all want to be first. They want to be high up. Two of them ask for chief places in his kingdom. He tells them that he cannot grant their request. When the ten other apostles heard of the request which the two had made, the ten were indignant. This was because they themselves were ambitious — they wanted the places themselves. Jesus calls the twelve around him and says: "You know that the princes of the Gentiles exercise dominion over them, and they that are great exercise authority upon them. But it shall not be so among you: but whosoever will be great among you, let him be your minister; and whosoever will be chief among you let him be your servant." Here we get another note in the grace of humility. It is not only teachableness, freedom from vanity and ambition, but it is also a willingness to serve. A humble man is a man who is ready to make himself useful. A man of lowly spirit is a man who will help his brethren, and here again Jesus in substance says; "Come unto me, for I am meek and lowly in heart. Whosoever will be chief among you let him be your servant, even as the Son of Man came not to be ministered unto but to minister, and to give his life a ransom for many." Does this not paint the picture of his life? As an inspired apostle puts it, "He went about doing good." He never patronized, nor looked down. He made himself of no reputation if only he could help those that needed help. He did not underestimate his powers, or make himself small, or feel himself to be unworthy; he simply came down to where men were in order to do them good. That is Christian humility.

The third lesson in humility was given his disciples on the very night of his betrayal, in the upper chamber. You will find the incident recorded in the thirteenth chapter of the Gospel according to St. John. The disciples are still filled with the ambitious spirit. They have not yet learned the joy of serving, for all have nettled hearts because they have not gotten the places which they wanted, and Jesus unwilling to allow the feast to go forward arises from the table, and taking a basin and girding himself with a towel proceeds to rinse the dust from the disciples' feet. Knowing their dulness of understanding he goes on to explain the meaning of his action, telling them, just as he has been willing to do the work of a slave in order to serve them, so they also must be willing to serve one another. Here, again, we see what humility really is. It is laying aside one's dignity, it is making one's self of no reputation, it is a willingness to come down, it is a delight in rendering service. And why was it that Jesus was able to do this? St. John gives the explanation in the wonderful words, "Knowing that he came from God, and was going back to God." It was not because he had mean ideas of himself, nor because he desired to make himself small; it was because he knew his divine origin and his divine destiny, and was conscious of his lofty position that he was willing to take the basin and the towel and do the work of a slave. This is the secret of humility everywhere and always. A man is never humble except by coming close to God. It is by thinking of the Eternal that man becomes willing to do the things which otherwise would be difficult or impossible. It is because we do not know that we have come from God, and forget that we are going back to Him that we make such an ado about our dignity, and prize so highly our reputation, and are so lordly and so lofty minded, and take such delight in putting on airs. Only he who is sure of God possesses the secret of humility.

How far Christian humility is removed from the miserable caricature of humility of which we have seen more than enough. Much of the so-called humility of the world is not humility at all. It is a slimy, crawling, despicable, snaky thing, a compound of vanity and falsehood. People who say they do not amount to anything, they cannot do anything, they have no talent, they do not know anything — never speak the truth. They do not try to speak the truth, they know they are not speaking the truth. It is their egotism which is masquerading under the form of humility. There is no vainer form of vanity than just that vanity which apes humility. The humility which Jesus wants, and which he exemplified in his life, is a form of strength. Only the strong man can be really humble. It is willingness to lay aside one's rights, it is a refusal to use one's power, it is a readiness to come down and to make one's self of no reputation. Jesus was always giving up his rights, he was always refusing to use his power. Repeatedly he had the opportunity to wreak vengeance on his enemies, but he would not do it because he was so humble. Hanging on the cross his enemies taunted him, saying, "Let him save himself." When they saw he would not save himself they supposed of course he did not because he could not, and they broke out in hateful jeers, "He saved others, himself he cannot save." But they were mistaken. He had the power to save himself, he would not use it. He could have called twelve legions of angels, but he would not call them. He was meek and lowly of heart, and was willing to give his life a ransom for many. St. Paul when he thinks of that which is most divine in

Jesus thinks of his grace of humility. Notwithstanding his exalted position, Paul reminds his Philippian converts that Jesus "made himself of no reputation and became obedient unto death, even the death of the cross. And therefore hath God highly exalted him and given him a name which is above every name, that at the name of Jesus every knee shall bow, and every tongue confess that he is Lord indeed."

XXI: THE PATIENCE OF JESUS

"A bruised reed shall he not break."
— Matthew xii: 20.

Let us think about the patience of Jesus. It will be better to deal first with the word. Of course everybody knows what patience is — at least he thinks he does — and yet somehow the very simplest words, and those with which we are most familiar, have a fashion of being misunderstood and of eluding us when we try to catch them and compel them to give up their meaning. Patience is one of the common words of every man s vocabulary, even though it may not be one of his most conspicuous virtues. Do we not say: "My patience was completely exhausted," "I have no patience with such a man," "My patience was never so tried in all my life," and of course we always understand what we mean when we use such language. What, then, does patience mean? We may discover that this old familiar word has more than one meaning. Words are sometimes like stars. You see a star shining in the sky, and to your eye it is a single star. The astronomer brings his telescope and to your amazement it is not a single star but a double star, two blazing suns have united their forces to produce that shining point of light in the blue. Just so there are words which shine like stars in the firmament of speech, single stars they seem until we subject them to scrutiny, when we discover that two meanings burn within the limits of their narrow syllables. This word "patience" is not a single but a double star. First of all it means: calmly waiting for something hoped for. In this sense even the animals are endowed with the virtue of patience. See the cat watching hour after hour, waiting for the appearance of a rat. She scarcely moves a hair and hardly winks an eye, waiting calmly for that happy moment when her victim shall appear. And just that virtue of imperturbable waiting is one of the great virtues of the human soul. Men have it in greater or less degrees, and sometimes it mounts to the level of genius. Blessed is the man who knows how to possess his soul in patience, waiting with unruffled mind for something hoped for. We find this virtue in every department of human life. Men make use of it in the building of their fortunes. A man invests his money in a piece of timber land which will bring him no returns for many years. The trees are small, and it may be that a third of a century must elapse before the trees are ready for the sawmill. But the man invests his money and calmly waits through the years, knowing that at the end of life he will be rich.

But this meaning does not exhaust the significance of patience. See yonder woman tortured by disease, she has been an invalid for years and in all this time she has never cried aloud, never complained, never rebelled against her fate. Here, indeed, we have something different from what we had in the preceding cases — and yet we call this patience, we look upon the woman in admiration, almost in awe, saying, "I never saw such patience in all my life." Or look at yonder man at the head of a great reformatory movement. He is endeavoring to bring to pass some mighty change in church or state or in society, and he has met with opposition at every step. For a while he makes progress, and then the way is blocked. Enemies multiply, friends forsake him, hearts grow cold, he is misunderstood, misrepresented, maligned, and hated. But, nevertheless, he goes bravely on, unsoured by opposition, undaunted by vituperation, never complaining, always hoping, bearing rebuff and reproof and criticism without a whine or a protest. Here again is patience. What is patience? It is the uncomplaining endurance of tribulation. These, then, are the two ideas which bum within the limits of our word "patience." First, it is the calm waiting for something hoped for; second, it is the unruffled endurance of pain and trouble. It is a temper of the soul, a temper that endures, waits, holds on. A man may have one sort of patience and not the other He may have the ability which calmly waits for something hoped for, and be quite impatient under the affliction of bodily pain or social persecution. On the other hand, he may be calm as a marble statue under physical infirmities, and may stand undaunted against all forms of social opposition and still be unable to wait steadfastly through the years for the accomplishment of a vast design. Patience exists in all degrees and grades. You have heard of the patience of Job. His is one of the immortal experiences of history. But how imperfect it was. His patience was the waiting for something hoped for, but it was not calm waiting; his patience was the endurance of tribulation, but it was not an endurance that refused to complain. He bewailed his fate, he groaned, he shrieked, he cursed the day on which he was born, he plunged and bellowed in his agony; but nevertheless he endured, he held on, he never surrendered. And it is this temper of endurance which constitutes the very heart and soul of patience, so that notwithstanding his manifold imperfections. Job stands among the heroes whose names shall never die. But would you see patience in both its forms raised to its highest power without a defect and without a flaw, you will find it in Jesus of Nazareth.

If patience means the calm waiting for something hoped for, then Jesus had this in a superlative degree. Was any waiting ever like his? He waited in a little country town in Galilee for thirty years before he entered into the work he felt God had given him to do. We do not always stop to ask ourselves how much this must have cost him. We Americans are among the most impatient of all people. It is difficult to induce many of our young men to wait long enough to prepare themselves adequately for the business of life. Thousands of boys drop out of school in the grammar grades not because they could not finish their education, but because they are impatient to go to work. Of the young men who go to the universities many drop out at the end of the Freshman year, others at the end of the Sophomore, others at the end of the Junior. Only a fraction of those who matriculate ever receive their diplomas, so impetuous are American youths, so eager are they to plunge into life's tumult and battle. It is an ever present question, therefore, in America how to shorten the curricula and how to devise short cuts to success and fortune. All sorts of schools and institutions have sprung up which give but partial training. These schools are patronized by young men who are impatient to get on. Now this impatience is often indicative of extraordinary vitality in the blood. Men are so full of life, so eager to help in doing the world's work, they cannot submit to the interminable delays which the traditional education involves. Think of what delay must have meant to Jesus. How his blood must have boiled in little sleepy Nazareth as he dreamed of the mighty things which ought to be done and which he felt he could do in the great arena. As man after man brushed by him on his way to success and renown his soul must have been agitated, he too must have felt the fever to hasten on. Think of what his dream was and you will understand how it must have tugged at him and made the years seem interminable in drowsy, prosaic Nazareth. But he waited. At twenty-one he said, Not yet. At twenty-five, Not yet. At twenty-eight, Not yet. It is in the twenties that the blood is hottest and the soul is most eager to get on. Through all the blazing years of youth Jesus waited in Nazareth. It was not until he was in his thirtieth year that he said to himself, The time has come.

A man at thirty is more than one-third of the way through life, and since Jesus has so much to do, certainly now that he has been baptized he will plunge into his work with alacrity, and push his projects with a vigor which will startle his contemporaries. Not so. He will calmly meditate on the best ways of helping his day and generation. The leaders of the people were looking for a man who would imitate the methods of the men who had hitherto proved themselves masters of the destinies of nations. It was clear to every eye that by means of the sword the finest execution could be done; that by military power the greatest results could be most speedily achieved; that by political genius established wrongs could be unthroned and defeated, and rights could be exalted. Jesus listened to these voices, they came up from all directions thundering in his ears. In imagination he saw himself on the top of a lofty mountain with the kingdoms of the world lying stretched out below him. He saw how he might gain possession of them by adopting methods employed by those who had lived before his day.

But having considered the whole situation he said, "No, I will not do what others have done, I will choose the slow and toilsome way; I will not cut the knot, I will untie it; I will not push the world, I will draw it; I will not subdue the world by military methods, I will heal it by the sympathy of human hearts." With this conviction firmly established in his soul he began his ministry in Galilee. To the men who stood around him he was always slow. "Why don't you go on? Why don't you hurry? Why don't you bring things to pass? Why don't you say everything you are going to say? Why don't you do everything you are going to do? Why don't you do it now?" — those were the questions which were thrown at him by friends and enemies all along the way. But when they urged him to hurry, his reply was, "Are there not twelve hours in the day?" or, "My hour is not yet come." And instead of setting all the land afire he tried, so it seemed, to suppress himself, to hold his disciples back, to keep his name from becoming glorious. When he healed sick men he said to them, "Tell no man."

When his disciples saw him all radiant on the mountain he cautioned them to keep still. The result was that at the end of his life he had made only one hundred and twenty disciples. What a pitiful outcome of a life so arduous, of work so strenuous and so unceasing! But the sight of a hundred and twenty men did not daunt him, he died with contentment in his heart. "Be of good cheer, I have overcome the world.' When? Not then, not a hundred years after his death, nor a thousand years, nor ten thousand years after. Nevertheless he has the tone of victory in his voice, knowing that in spite of all the obstacles, delays, and retrogressions, the outcome is absolutely certain. Before Pontius Pilate, the Roman procurator, he says, "To this end was I born and for this cause came I into the world, that I should bear witness unto the truth." He did his work and died. The progress has been slow, but his patient heart is still untroubled, and from his throne of glory he looks upon the slow-moving ages, patient with the feeble efforts of his followers, willing to wait for the reluctant submission of rebellious hearts, knowing that by and by, sometime, somewhere, the kingdom will be established and all his dreams fulfilled. That is patience at its climax.

But this does not exhaust the patience of Jesus. The way of a reformer is never smooth, and the way which Jesus traveled was the thorniest which human feet have ever trod. It was literal truth that he came unto his own and his own received him not, the light shone in the darkness but the darkness comprehended it not. With a love that caused his heart to glow he knocked at the door in Jerusalem, but the men who kept the door refused to open it. He knocked at the door in Nazareth, the door was opened and then shut in his face. He traveled throughout Galilee, and in city after city he met with nothing but repulse; but he was never discouraged, he never complained. Wherever he went he was pursued by men who were his enemies. They watched him in order that they might trip him. They questioned him in order that they might get him into a trap. How difficult it is to speak if one is speaking in the presence of people who are watching each sentence, determined if possible to catch the speaker in an error. Wherever he went his conduct was scrutinized by eyes that were green with envy. Everything he did was criticised, every action called forth a storm of fresh abuse. His enemies gathered around him like a swarm of mosquitoes biting him, like a swarm of hornets stinging him — but he never complained. They nagged at him, pelted him with abusive epithets, sowed the land with lies about him, but he never grew bitter. We have known many a good man to grow sour simply because he had been misunderstood by a few people. Many a good woman has grown bitter because of unfortunate experiences with those who were her fellow-workers in the church. This Man of Galilee knew little but misunderstanding and ingratitude and criticism and abuse; but he never complained and at the end of the day he was as sweet as at dawn. Long before he came somebody had said that when the supreme man arrived he would submit to tribulation without complaining. As men looked upon this Man of Galilee they were reminded of the great line of the prophet, "As a lamb before the shearer is dumb, so he opened not his mouth." And if Jesus was patient with his enemies he was equally patient with his friends, and probably his friends tried him no less sorely than his enemies. His friends did not understand him. His own mother and brothers were not in sympathy with him. The disciples to whom he gave himself with a devotion that has never been equalled were constantly failing to catch the import of the things he told them. They were slow and stupid, petty and selfish, unable to take in the great things he had to say — but he was patient with them. Even on the last night of his earthly life, when he met them in a private house in Jerusalem to have a last talk with them, they quarrelled among themselves as to their places at the table. But even this brings from him no more than an affectionate rebuke. He simply takes a basin of water and performs the work which was ordinarily performed by slaves, rinsing the dust from their unsandalled feet, — by this act teaching what he had been trying to teach them from the beginning, that he who would be greatest must be the servant of all. There is a beautiful quotation in the Old Testament which the apostle Matthew has put at the centre of his Gospel, throwing a flood of light upon the impression which Jesus made upon those who came nearest to him. After he had vanished from their sight, the beauty of his character came up before them as they had never been able to see it in the days of his humiliation, and among the beautiful portraits which men in preceding generations had sketched of an ideal character Matthew felt that not one more fully portrayed Jesus of Nazareth than this one, "A bruised reed he shall not break, and smoking flax he shall not quench." This was his temper whether he was dealing with foes or friends. He demanded much of his disciples, but he did not demand it all at once. He kept saying if a man has even a little faith, even so small as a grain of mustard seed, he has enough to start with, and by means of this he will be able to work wonders. Great men have oftentimes been notoriously impatient with their weaker and more incompetent brethren; strong themselves they could not sympathize with weakness; clear in their own conceptions they could not endure the stupidity of those who floundered in mist and fog. The bruised reed they had no use for, the smoking wick they despised and quenched. But the patient Man of Galilee had a temper altogether different. He sympathized with weakness, he was considerate of mental dulness, he was long-suffering in the presence of moral awkwardness. Even a bruised reed he would not break, and even a smoking wick he would coax back into flame.

And ever since Jesus lived and taught, men have loved to think that God is patient. To every follower of Jesus the Almighty is a long-suffering God. He has vast plans running through the ages, and He is willing to wait for their fulfilment. Men look around them at the woe and havoc, the suffering and the tragedy, and say: "How could God ever make a world like this? How can He endure it to have these things go on?" They do not understand that He is patient, infinitely patient, and is willing to wait until human hearts surrender, and by their obedience bring the long and bitter night to an end. Not only does He wait, but He also suffers indignity at our hands without blazing up in anger and consuming us. We may be ungrateful, insolent, irreverent, rebellious; we may refuse to do the things He asks us to do, and persist in doing the things that are contrary to His will; we may injure ourselves and hurt others, nevertheless He will not strike us down. He will give us yet another day, and still another, saying, "Perhaps to-morrow the sin will be repented of and the prodigal will come home."

XXII: THE COURAGE OF JESUS

"Fear not."
— Luke V: 10.

He who speaks of courage speaks of a live subject. It is a virtue which everybody admires and which everybody has admired from the beginning. There has never been a nation which did not admire courageous men. There is not an age known to history in which heroism has not been deemed a lovely and a precious thing. The old Egyptians gloried in their bravery, and so also did the Assyrians, the Babylonians, the Persians, the Macedonians, the Romans, and the Greeks; and the very quality which was rated so highly thousands of years before Jesus came is also gloried in by the Boers of the nineteenth century and the Japanese of the twentieth. When we deal, therefore, with courage we are dealing with a virtue which is not peculiar to any race, or confined to any generation, or deemed a virtue by any one religion. It is one of the elemental tempers of the human spirit, one of the foundation stones in the great structure of character, one of the shining qualities of the wonderful being who is known as man. Is there a man so base that he does not covet courage? Is there one so low he would not be proud to be counted brave? There are only three words in our English speech which pierce the heart to the very centre: one is thief, the second is liar, the third is coward. Coward is the most damning of them all.

When we come, therefore, to the study of the ideal man we might expect to find him giving us a wonderful exhibition of courage. And this is indeed what we find: in Jesus of Nazareth we find bravery at its best, courage at its loftiest, heroism at its climax.

There are different kinds of courage. There is a courage which we may call physical. It runs in the blood, it is a kind of instinct. This sort of courage is not peculiar to man, it is possessed also by the brutes. The bulldog has it and so also has the weasel. It is possessed by man in all the stages of his development. It is an indifference to danger, a contempt for suffering and for death. But the courage of Jesus was not this. His was a higher and nobler possession. His was the courage of the mind, the heroism of the heart. It was a sober and reasoned thing. He deliberately counted the cost and paid it. Nor was his courage military. Military courage is the most common of all forms of courage in the world, and one of the earliest developed. Military courage is the courage which the soldier has in the time of battle. In time of battle men move in masses, the very momentum of the movement carries them onward. There is an excitement in battle which thrills the nerves and heats the blood; men are beside themselves, and are carried forward by forces which are not their own. The courage of war is spectacular, appealing to the eye because the paraphernalia of war is splendid, the waving flag, the fife and drum, the glittering steel, the measured tread of marching men — all this assists the heart to scoff at danger and to mock at death. But splendid as this is it is common and has always been abundant. The lowest races possess it as highly developed as the highest. You never can get courage going beyond the military courage which the Japanese displayed in the recent war. And that courage was not a whit superior to the courage displayed at Gettysburg, and the courage at Gettysburg was not a bit finer than the courage at Bunker Hill and Waterloo, and that did not surpass the courage at Thermopylae, nor did that outstrip the courage manifested by the Indian braves who laughed at death on this island before Henry Hudson sailed up the river which now bears his name. There never has been an advance in military courage since the world began. From the very beginning the courage of battle has been full-statured and complete. The courage of our Lord was not military, it was the courage which manifested itself in isolation. There was nobody to march with him. He marched alone. Palestine was filled with evils, he alone was brave enough to strike them. Injustice lifted its hideous head, and he alone resisted it. Hypocrisy made a mockery of religion, and he alone stabbed it. He trod the winepress alone. Even the men whom he succeeded in attracting to him left him and fled at the final hour. But even then he did not wince or falter, saying, "I am alone and yet not alone, for the Father is with me."

There is also such a thing as occasional courage, — courage that is born of some feverish moment, drawn from the heart by some overwhelming disaster. This is the courage which we see displayed in time of a great fire, or of a great flood, or of a great wreck on the sea. What splendid deeds of daring firemen do in rescuing men and women from burning buildings at the risk of their own lives! How it thrills the blood to see men leap into the life-boat, and make their way out over the angry sea and rescue the sailors clinging to the rigging of a sinking ship! This is courage which is indeed sublime, but it is not equal to the courage of repose. Disaster heats the blood and kindles a fire in the mind which makes it easy for the soul to dare great things; but the courage of Jesus of Nazareth was the courage of the quiet and commonplace days, courage that had to be manifested hour by hour along the dusty road when there was nothing to heat the blood or stir the mind to lofty moods.

If you were to paint Jesus as a hero, in what situation would you sketch him? Would you think of him on that great day on which he cleansed the Temple, driving out the cattle, overturning the tables of the money-changers, saying to sellers of doves, "Take these things hence"? Would you paint him as he appeared when in the streets of Jerusalem he stood up and faced his implacable foes, the Scribes and Pharisees, and hurled at them sentences which at the distance of nineteen hundred years still smoke like thunderbolts? Or would you paint him as he came from the Garden of Gethsemane and startled the band of men who have come to arrest him by saying, "I am the man you seek"? Or would you picture him going to Golgotha saying to the women who bewailed his fate, "Weep not for me, but for yourselves and your children weep"? All these situations I admit are picturesque and thrilling. Every reader of the New Testament catches them up and holds them forever in his memory. In each one of them we see heroism in a high and lovely form, but these are not the scenes to which I call your attention at the present moment.

Would you ask me to give you an illustration of the courage of Jesus' heart, I would take you first of all to Nazareth on that day on which for the first time he announced his mission to the men and women who had known him from boyhood. It was necessary for him to say things which would offend, and he said them. He was to preach the truth, but he could not preach the truth without cutting across the grain of the prejudices of these people. He went calmly onward, however, and preached the truth. To estrange the hearts of those who have known and esteemed us for many years, to cut one's self off from the respect and sympathy and love of those in whose friendship we have found solace and delight — that is hard indeed. And that is what Jesus did on that awful day in Nazareth. By the simple speaking of the truth he alienated from him the minds and hearts of the people in whose midst he had grown to manhood and whose high regard had been one of the most valuable of all his earthly treasures. He was a courageous man that day, and equally courageous was he in the streets of Capernaum when he talked to that crowd of five thousand men whom he had fed a little while before in the desert beyond the Sea of Galilee. He came into the world to bear witness to the truth, but men were not willing to receive it. At the beginning of his address every one was enthusiastic, but as he spoke the great crowd began to melt away. The five thousand dwindled down to four thousand, the four thousand decreased to three thousand, the three thousand sank to two thousand, the two thousand became one thousand, the one thousand fell to five hundred, the five hundred to one hundred, the one hundred to fifty, the fifty to twenty-five, and these at last became twenty, the twenty dwindled to fifteen, and at last only twelve men stood beside him, and these twelve had such doleful, wavering faces that he said to them, "Will ye also go away?" What is there harder in this world than that? A religious teacher finds his joy in the ears and hearts of those who hear him. To hold them, to teach them, to inspire them — this is indeed his glory, his all. But to teach the truth and go on teaching it even though the congregation grows less and less and less, that requires the forthputting of the very highest temper of the soul. It was just that kind of courage which Jesus had. The courage which he manifested in Capernaum was manifested everywhere.

It is not an easy thing to offend society and to offend it in such a way as to lose caste and standing. The people in Jesus' day were great sticklers for forms of fasting. Jesus minimized the value of them. They were exceedingly scrupulous in regard to sabbatical laws. Jesus could not keep them, he did not believe in keeping them. They were punctilious in regard to the number of times they washed their hands before they sat down to eat. Jesus had no time for such elaborate foolery. The best people of his day divided things into clean and unclean, people into clean and unclean — Jesus could pay no attention to these distinctions. All men were his brethren, and so he associated with people who had lost caste. By so doing he lost his own reputation. Has any one courage enough here to do that? He went contrary to the established usages of the best society of his day; he trampled on conventionalities which were counted sacred as the law of the Eternal. And the result was he was suspected, shunned, and abhorred. But he did even more than this: he surrendered the good opinion which many of the people had formed of him. When he first appeared the air was filled with applause, men looked upon him as the promised Messiah. The land blazed with enthusiasm. The people had certain ideals, and Jesus could not conform to them. They had fixed ideas, and Jesus could not carry them out. He threw cold water upon these fires of enthusiasm and they died down lower and lower, until at last there was nothing but a great stretch of smoldering ashes, and he stood in the centre of the ashes the most forsaken and hated of men. It takes tremendous courage to lay aside one's reputation, and also to forego the bliss of popular applause. But he did a braver thing even than this: he gave up the good opinion of the best people of his day. He was reverent, religious, sensitive, but there were certain things it was necessary for him to say because they were true things, and he said them. By saying them he exposed himself to the charge of being a blasphemer, but he said them. He was willing to do his duty even though by the doing of it he won for himself the ignominy of being counted a blasphemer, a lunatic, and a traitor.

Only the very loftiest heroism can meet such a test as that. But we have not yet reached the climax. If it is difficult for a man to withstand his enemies, much more difficult is it for him to withstand his friends. There are many men who can resist the people who are opposed to them who cannot withstand the opinions and wishes of their friends. Many of us can pour denunciation on the men who hate us, but we succumb at once to the gracious words of those who wish us well. Peter was Jesus' dearest friend; but when Peter on a certain occasion says to him, "Far be it from thee, Lord, this shall never happen unto thee," quick as a flash the reply comes, "Get thee behind me, Satan." James and John present what seems to them a most reasonable request — Jesus says, "I cannot grant this." Judas was one of the most trusted of the apostolic company — so trusted that he was made the treasurer of the band; but Jesus by the simple telling of the truth and the living of a perfect life estranged the affections of this man until at last he became his betrayer. Many of you have courage sufficient to stand against your enemies, how many of you can resist the influence and wishes of your friends?

But if you want illustrations of the courage of Jesus, you must take the entire New Testament, for all the Gospels are a portrait of a hero. The story of Jesus' life is the most heroic record ever written, and any man who wishes to increase the bravery of his heart must read this book day and night. See him as he sets his face steadfastly to go to Jerusalem, where he knows they are going to scourge him and spit upon him and kill him. His friends endeavor to dissuade him, they strive to hold him back. He keeps steadily on, knowing that at Jerusalem he will give his life a ransom for many. Lord Randolph Churchill, one of the most distinguished of Englishmen of the last century, in the year 1891 wrote a letter to his wife telling her that he had quit politics once and forever. He said: "More than two-thirds, in all probability, of my life is over, and I will not spend the remainder of my years in beating my head against a stone wall. There has been no consideration, no indulgence, no memory or gratitude — nothing but spite, malice, and abuse. I am quite tired and dead sick of it all, and will not continue political life any longer." How natural, how human that sounds! Haven't you heard men say it? Possibly some of you have said it yourself. You have engaged in some reform, and have been misrepresented and abused. You have turned away, saying, "I am tired, I am sick." Maybe you were a worker in the church; you were misrepresented, you were thwarted; you cast up your work, saying, "I am tired, I am sick." Why do men talk thus? Because they are cowards. Only cowards surrender, only cowards get tired and sick. Jesus steadfastly set his face to go to Jerusalem and never turned back until he reached the cross. See him as he goes onward, trampling on all the precious things of earth, putting under his feet the ambitions by which the hearts of other men are fired, trampling into the dust the prizes and the joys of life. Make out a list of the things which you count most valuable and worth while, and you will see that Jesus placed every one of them beneath his feet. With the tread of a conqueror he goes on to his death, saying, "I do always those things that are pleasing unto Him."

And yet his courage never overleaps itself and becomes audacity or recklessness. Some men have found fault with him because on certain occasions he escaped and hid himself. He retired into out-of-the way places, not because he was a coward, but because he was so brave. It is easier to die than to live a life such as Jesus lived. He hid himself sometimes to escape the fury of his enemies, because he desired to remain a little longer in order that he might establish in men's hearts the truths that would redeem the world. Thousands of men every year leap off this planet by self-destruction. They do it because they are cowards. Jesus bore the burden and endured the cross until his work had been completed. And so with such a temper we are not surprised to find him at every stage of his trial acting like the hero that he was. When the soldiers buffeted him and cuffed him, cursed him and spat upon him, he never said a word. He was so courageous that he dared to be silent. As a sheep before her shearers is dumb, so he opened not his mouth.

When he comes at last to stand before Pontius Pilate, he stands so erect that Pilate is afraid of him, and the heart of the Roman procurator flutters when Jesus says to him, "For this cause was I born, unto this end came I into the world, to bear witness to the truth." And when at last they nail him to the cross the only thing he will say is, "Father, forgive them, for they know not what they do." Rousseau was right when he wrote his immortal line, "If the life and death of Socrates were those of a sage, the life and death of Jesus are those of a God."

XXIII: THE INDIGNATION OF JESUS

"And when he had looked round about on them with anger."
— Mark iii: 5.

There are certain moods and feelings which we are reluctant to ascribe to Jesus, because they are so common and so human. Characteristics which are conspicuous and disconcerting in ourselves, we do not readily associate with him. For instance, was it possible for Jesus to be angry? If it was, he was amazingly like ourselves. The humblest and least gifted of us are adepts in the realm of indignation. Our capacity for wrath was manifested in us early, and we have developed it by constant use. No emotion is more nearly universal and none is more easily aroused. The very universality of the experience makes us reluctant to attribute it to one who is at so many points above us, and whose life, however like our own, has in it so many things which are unique.

Moreover, anger is associated in our mind with infirmity. Much of our own anger has been of the earth earthy. It has been a boiling of the blood, full of sound and fury, having no ethical significance. Sometimes it has been a burst of petulance, an explosion of nervous energy, a sort of madness bordering on the frontiers of insanity. While the fever was upon us we felt our wrath was justifiable, but on the cooling of the blood we repented in sackcloth and ashes. We have also noticed what anger does for others. It has not escaped us that when men and women are angry they usually make fools of themselves. This fact has made a deep impression on us. Most of the indignation which we have known has been so childish or so brutish, so full of fury and of bitterness, that we find it hard to give it place in the experience of a strong and holy man. So prone is anger to mix itself with base and unlovely elements, and so frequently does it stir up the mud at the bottom of the soul, that it has been often classed among the vices as a passion which is always ignoble, and therefore to be condemned, resisted, strangled. It was thus that the Stoics taught, contending that ever to be moved by anger is a sign of weakness and unworthy of a full-grown man. The philosophy of the Stoics is not consciously accepted by us, but the considerations which led them to their estimate of anger are still operative in us all. It is not easy to free one's self from the feeling that anger has something sinful in it, or that if anger is not actually sinful, it is at any rate unlovely, a defect or flaw in conduct, a deformity in character from which the lovers of the beautiful and good may wisely pray to be delivered. It is because of this assumption that anger is in its essence sinful that many persons find it impossible to think of Jesus in an angry mood. When the New Testament says that he was angry they glide over the sentence hurriedly, giving the words a Pickwickian sense, and breathe more freely when they have come out again into a paragraph which portrays his tenderness and love. Once decide that anger is a sinful or an animal passion, and you must deny it a place in the portrait of an ideal man.

But the evangelists were not Stoics, and they were not handicapped by the notions which bewilder us. They felt that they must write down clearly what they saw and heard, and prompted thus to tell a round, unvarnished tale they do not hesitate to inform us that Jesus sometimes blazed with anger. The blast of his scorn was so hot that it frightened and scorched those on whom it fell. They tell us that it was inhumanity and insincerity which always kindled his heart to furnace heat. When he saw men — ordained religious leaders of the people — more interested in their petty regulations than in the welfare of their fellow-men, his eyes burned with holy fire. Those who were present never forgot the flash of his eye as he slowly looked round upon the pedants whose hardness of heart he held in abhorrence. He despised the lying superstitions which had accumulated around the idea of death, and loathed the mummery which attended the burial of the dead. The hollow bowlings of paid mourners in the presence of the holy mystery of death aroused his soul to indignant protest. Any darkening of the world by cruelty or craft brought his soul to its feet fiery-eyed and defiant. He was angered by the desecration of the Temple. The sordid wretches who cared nothing for anthems and prayers and everything for money, kindled a fire in him which well-nigh consumed him. The miscreants who fled before him had never seen such a flame as darted from his eyes. That a building erected for the purpose of adorning the name of God should be converted into a market was so abhorrent to his great soul that he was swept onward into action which astounded his disciples and which has been to many a scandal ever since. No one can understand the cleansing of the Temple who has never experienced the force and heat of righteous indignation. There are many sentences from his lips which after the lapse of nineteen hundred years still burn with fervent heat. Who can read the parable of Dives and Lazarus without feeling the fire of a holy scorn? Who can read the denunciation of the Pharisees without realizing that he is in the presence of a volcano belching molten lava? No one could speak language like that which the evangelists have recorded who was not capable of tremendous indignation. It is a wrath which leaps beyond the wrath of man. It is the very wrath of God Himself. One of the purposes of the New Testament is to give us a new revelation of anger. Take away Jesus' capacity for indignation and you destroy the Jesus of the Gospels. His anger was one of the powers by which he did his work. His blazing wrath is one of the most glorious features of his character. Had he been less emotional, he would not have stirred men as he did. Had his passion been less intense, the world would never have called him "Master."

Here, then, we have in Jesus what seems to some a contradiction. He is a Lamb and at the same time he is the Lion of the Tribe of Judah. He caresses like a mother and he also strikes like a thunderbolt. He is tender but he is also terrible; he is loving but he also smites with a blow which crushes. How can we reconcile the indignation of Jesus with his love? Nothing is easier. His indignation is the creation of his love. His wrath proceeds from his holiness. His mercy would have no meaning were it not for his immeasurable capacity for anger. Take away his indignation and you destroy the basis of his holiness, his righteousness, his mercy, and his love. Love and indignation are not antagonists or rivals. They ever go together, each one unable to live without the other. Only those who have? never loved have difficulty in understanding the heart's capacity for wrath. Did you ever see a love stand calm-eyed and gentle-tempered in the presence of the villain who had dared insult the queen of his heart? When since the world began has love ever maintained a quiet pulse in the presence of the assailant of the loved one? A mother, all gentleness and sweetness as she moves among her children, passes into an avenging fury in the face of a foe who attempts to harm them. The dimensions of her indignation will be determined by the depth and heat of her love. It is the hottest love which when enlisted in the welfare of others scorches opposing forces to cinders. The power of loving and the power of hating must always go together. There is right and there is wrong, the first must be approved, the second must be condemned. The condemnation must not be cold but vehement. It must carry with it all the energy of the soul. It must have at the heart of it that heavenly fire which is known on earth as indignation.

In Jesus, then, we see what a normal man is and feels. He is full-orbed, complete. He gives sweep to every passion of the soul. He will not admit that in the garden of the heart there are any plants which the Heavenly Father has planted which ought to be rooted up. All the impulses, desires, and passions with which the Almighty has endowed us have a mission to perform, and life's task is not to strangle them but to train them for their work.

Jesus was angry but he did not sin. Anger because of its heat readily passes beyond its appointed limits. Like all kinds of fire, it is dangerous and difficult to control. But Jesus controlled it. "Thus far," he said, "and no farther." No sinful element mingled in that indignation which burned with a white and resistless heat. The irritation which we so often feel, the exasperation which lacerates and rends the heart, the bitterness of which we are ashamed — all these were absent from Jesus' anger. His wrath was the hottest ever known upon our earth, but the heart in which it burned was sinless. Our anger is frequently a manifestation of our selfishness. We become indignant over trifles. The street-car does not stop, or somebody carelessly knocks off our hat, or a servant disappoints us, and we are all aflame. Our comfort has been molested, our rights have been entrenched upon, our dignity has been affronted, and we are downright mad. Ravellings and shavings can set us blazing. But in the presence of gigantic outrages perpetrated on the helpless and the weak, some of us are as calm as a summer morning. Bad men do not make us angry unless they interfere with our own personal affairs. If they wrong others we will make excuses for them, and cover them all over with the down of extenuating syllables, saying, "Poor men, they are more sinned against than sinning, they are the products of the age, the victims of the system," and thus do we take from guilt its heinousness by the flattering smile of a placid face.

Our indignation then is quite different from that of Jesus. His anger never had its roots in selfishness. When men abused him, he was unruffled. When they lied about him, his pulse beat was not quickened. When they nailed his hands to the cross, no trace of anger darkened his face. His calm lips kept on praying, "Forgive them, for they know not what they do." It was when he saw his brother men abused that his great soul rose in wrath. The more helpless the person who was mistreated, the hotter was the fire of his indignation. Against rich people who imposed upon the poor, and against clever people who took advantage of the ignorant, and against strong people who mistreated the weak, and against crafty people who laid traps for the innocent, his soul blazed with a heat which became an imperishable and awe-inspiring memory in the apostolic church. It was when he saw cruelty perpetrated on the defenceless that his indignation rose to the fury of a tempest. The thought of bad men leading innocent souls to sin, converted him into a furnace of fire. What a whirlwind of flame sweeps through a sentence like this, "Whoso shall cause one of these little ones which believe on me to stumble, it is profitable for him that a great mill-stone should be hanged about his neck, and that he should be sunk in the depth of the sea." Tender, indeed, must have been the heart from which could come such forked lightnings! If, then, we have ever been scandalized by the account of Jesus' indignation, we should examine ourselves and find out why we shrink from the thought that a man like him should burn with anger. Whenever we find in Jesus a word or deed which seems to us to be a departure from what we conceive to be the standard of absolute rectitude, it is well to pause and study our standards of rectitude afresh, for it may be that what we conceive to be a defect in him may reveal to us a limitation in ourself. If we find fault with him because he blazed with anger, it may be that our criticism springs from blood which has become impoverished. If we fail to bum in the presence of cruelty and injustice, it is because the higher faculties of the soul have become atrophied by sin. If wood does not bum, it is because it is green or rotten. If hearts do not burn with holy fire against wicked men and their wicked deeds, it is because the heart is too undeveloped to feel what manly hearts were meant to feel, or because the core of the heart has been eaten out by the base practices of a godless life.

It is one of the lamentable signs of our times — our incapacity for anger. Many of us are lukewarm in the presence of evils which are colossal. Some of us are indifferent. Indifference to wrong-doing is always a sign of moral deterioration. If we do not flame against villainy, it is because there is so much of the villain in ourself. We would despise graft with a consuming detestation if our own palms were not so itching. The healthy soul resents and resists every form of wrong. The unspoiled heart goes out like a man in wrath against the forces of iniquity. Nothing is more needed in our day than enlarged capacity for moral indignation. Nothing so clears the atmosphere as the heat of hearts heated by holy anger. There are evils so gigantic and so deeply rooted that nothing less than a thunderstorm will overwhelm them. Bad men will abound more and more unless good men hurl thunderbolts. Criminals become brazen, wrong-doers walk insolently, rascals take possession of high places, until good men, aflame with indignation, arise and sweep them from the seats of power. Society would be cleansed of much of its pollution if we had more men and women capable of becoming genuinely angry. Let us pray then every day that a new indignation may sweep through the world. As Plutarch put it long ago, "Anger is one of the winds by which the sails of the soul are filled." Many a belated bark would have reached port long ago if anger had been allowed to do its perfect work. It is the devil's trick to keep good men from becoming angry. Not only are we permitted as Christians to be angry, but it is our duty on occasion to allow this billow of fire to roll through the soul. Martin Luther is not the only man who has worked better when he was angry, and many of us limp to our task because we have lost one of the elements of moral power. He was a wise Englishman who wrote, "Anger is one of the sinews of the soul; he that wants it hath a maimed mind, and with Jacob sinew-shrunk in the hollow of his thigh must needs halt."

In the indignation of Jesus we get light upon the character of God. This man's anger flows from a fountain in the heart of the Eternal. The wrath of the Lamb" is, as we have been often reminded, a figure of speech, but like all Biblical figures of speech, it is a window opening out on the infinite. The anger of Jesus is a revelation of the anger of God. It is significant that it is the beloved disciple and the man to whom tradition has ascribed a heart unusually loving and tender, who has most to say about the "wrath of the Lamb." As he brooded over the years of his intercourse with Jesus, there was one trait which rose before him again and again, and that was the anger of Jesus. When he speaks of it, it is always with syllables which hush the heart. The man who declares that "God is love" is the man who exhorts us to fiee from the "wrath of the Lamb."

The New Testament is a glorious book. Its lines are straight, its discrimination is fine, it rings true. It is absolutely free from sentimentalism. It has no sickly fondness for bad people. It does not deal in excuses and in extenuations. It has no abnormal tenderness. The world is full of sentimentalists, — men and women who gush of love, and who do not know what love is. After listening to their flimsy talk it is refreshing to get into a book where every bad deed is held up to scorn and every bad man, if unrepentant, is overwhelmed with shame. Nowhere in the Gospels is there a soft or flabby thought, a doughy or mushy feeling. All is high and straight and fine and firm and true. Under such a sky, life becomes august, solemn, beautiful. It is worth while to strive, to work, to suffer. One feels sure that God is in His heaven, and that though wickedness may flourish for a season, God's heart burns with quenchless fire against it, and that at the end of the days every impure man, and every cruel man, and every man who loves and makes a lie, will find himself outside the city whose streets are gold and whose gates are pearl.

XXIV: THE REVERENCE OF JESUS

"Hallowed be thy name."
— Matthew vi: 9.

No analysis of the character of Jesus would be complete which failed to recognize his reverence. It is one of the traits which contribute most largely to his loveliness, a characteristic which attracts the notice of every observing mind. To write a definition of reverence is not easy. There are some things which the heart can sense but which the intellect cannot easily define. We know what reverence is, and yet we stumble in trying to define it. It is respect, regard, esteem, and honor; yes, and it is more than these. Those thin and pallid syllables do not express all which the heart feels when the word "reverence" is spoken. The basis of reverence is respect or honor, but it is respect or honor working with unwonted energy. It is a deep movement of the soul. It is respect or honor squared and cubed. And then again there is an elevation in the word "reverence" which respect and esteem do not have.

Reverence is respect and esteem moving at high altitudes. It is one of the loftiest of all the emotions of the soul, and that is why it eludes us when we try to capture it in the meshes of a definition. What is it? It is homage and obeisance and devotion, yes, and something more. It is awe and fear and adoration; yes, but even these do not tell the full-rounded story. The fact is, reverence is a complex emotion, made up of mingled feelings of the soul. There is in it respect and also affection and also fear, and along with these an abiding consciousness of dependence. There is probably no expression which defines what we mean by reverence so well as the Old Testament phrase, "The fear of the Lord." The wise men of Israel were convinced that the fear of the Lord is the beginning of wisdom. Their effort was to make men conscious of the existence of a God of infinite power and wisdom and goodness. He was the High and Holy One who inhabits eternity, and is therefore not to be approached carelessly or thought of lightly. The Temple in Jerusalem was built in such a way as to establish the fear of the Lord in the hearts of the people. Its architecture was continually reminding them that to be reverent is to be wise. Into the outer courts of the Temple every

Hebrew might go; into the inner court or holy place only one particular class of men could enter; while into the innermost sanctuary or holy of holies only one man was permitted to make his way, and that man only on one great day of the year. In this way the cardinal truth was promulgated that God is majestic and holy and can be approached only by a humble and prostrate heart. This fear of the Lord was mighty in Jesus. God was continually before his eyes. His soul was pervaded with the sense of His presence, and all that he said and did was bathed in an atmosphere created by this consciousness of the fellowship and favor of the Eternal.

To illustrate this is not easy. Jesus' entire life is an illustration of it. One cannot pick out isolated words or acts and hold them up, saying, "Behold, how reverent he was!" A man cannot be reverent at intervals. He must be reverent all the time or not at all. If he is reverent on Monday and not on Tuesday, then his Monday reverence was a pretence and a sham. Reverence is not a vesture which can be put on and laid off, it runs in the very blood of the soul. It is impossible to localize it. It is rather an atmosphere in which the personality is enveloped. It is a settled habit of the spirit, a fixed attitude of the heart, an unchanging trend of all the currents of the being toward God. No matter what Jesus is saying or doing, we feel we are in the presence of a reverential man. Would you see illustrations of his reverence, read the Gospels!

The earnestness with which he was always pleading for reverence in others is proof that in him reverence was a divine and indispensable possession. He could not have so loved it in others had he not possessed it himself. "When you pray, say. Our Father, hallowed be thy name." Probably no other words in the Lord's prayer have been so frequently slurred and overlooked as "hallowed be thy name." They lie, as it were, in the valley between the great name of God and the glorious Kingdom for which we are looking and waiting. We slide over them as though they were only a parenthesis, and hasten on to ask for bread and deliverance from our greatest foe. But Jesus is careful to place this petition at the very forefront of all our praying. Unless this desire is uppermost in our heart we are not in the mood of prayer. If our first thought is of ourselves and not of God, then we are not praying after the fashion of Jesus. When he tells us to put this petition first it is because he always put it first himself. It was his supreme ambition that his Father's name should be kept beautiful and holy. "When you pray, then," he said to his disciples, "pray that God's name may be consecrated, reverenced, kept holy; hedge it from the contaminating influences of an evil world, separate it from all other names which the lips speak or the mind thinks." Any low or unworthy thought of God was to Jesus' mind abhorrent and degrading. Living always with an eye single to the glory of God, he urged men everywhere so to speak and act and live that others seeing their good works might glorify their Father in heaven.

Holding God continually before his eyes he saw everything in relation to the Eternal. His respect for men was due not to what men were in themselves but to what they were in the eyes of God. They were God's children and therefore no matter how poor or degraded, they were worthy of respect and honor. Any cruelty in word or inhumanity in action toward a human being caused the heart of Jesus to flash fire, because such treatment of God's children was in his mind an insult to God Himself. His reverence for his Father made the whole world holy, and because of his adoration for the Creator he could not turn his back upon any created being. "Honor all men" was one of the earliest exhortations of the apostles. It had its roots running down into Jesus' immeasurable reverence for God.

How careful he was for the fair name of his Father is illustrated in what he says in regard to oaths. The religious leaders of his day had a certain form of reverence, but it was circumscribed and shallow. They reverenced the letters which spelled God's name so highly that they would never take them upon their lips. But they had no hesitation in filling the empty spaces with other words. If they would not swear in the name of God, they would fill their oaths with the names of things which God had made. Jesus' reverence for his Father was so intense that it extended also to the things created by his Father. The Jews were in the habit of swearing by heaven, but this to Jesus was profane because heaven was made by God. They sometimes swore by the earth, but this was to him also shocking because the earth belongs to God. Sometimes they swore by Jerusalem, but this also could not be permitted for it was a city dear to God. If they swore by their own heads, they were also in the wrong, for their head was created by the Almighty. Here is indeed a sensitive heart. He feels so keenly the majesty and dignity of the Eternal Father that all created things shine in the reflected glory of His face, and therefore nothing is to be treated irreverently, dragged down into vulgarity, or converted into a joke.

His reverence for the Temple was unfailing. Every stone in it spoke to him of God, and every ceremony celebrated within its courts had in it a meaning which soothed and comforted his heart. Any desecration of a building erected to promote God's glory was to him horrible and unendurable. It was in this building that eyes were to be opened and hearts cleansed to behold the King in His beauty. Around it clustered sacred associations and sweet memories of many years. It was to Jesus indeed a holy place. But not so to many of his' countrymen. In the process of moral degradation reverence is one of the first of the virtues to disappear. It is a flower of paradise which cannot blossom in the chill atmosphere of sordidness and vulgarity. The love of money had eaten out the hearts of many of Jesus' countrymen. They cared more for gain than they did for God. Caring nothing for God, why should they care for God's temple? They converted the temple courts into a market-place and drowned the anthems and the prayers with the clink of money and the bellowing of steers. Jesus could not endure it. Other men had endured it — he could not. Irreverence is a sword through the heart of a reverent man. Never did Jesus show such a tempest of emotion as in the cleansing of the Temple. To the onlookers he seemed to be beside himself. He became all at once an avenging fury, and before the miscreants knew what was happening their coins were rolling over the temple floor and their flocks and herds were in the street. The explanation of the tempest lies in these three words, — "My Father's house." It was not an ordinary house. It was the house of God. It was erected for God's worship. It was a shrine for the adoring heart. It was intended to be a solace for men's woes and troubles, the very gate of Heaven. "Take these things hence; make not my Father's house a house of merchandise." It was his reverence which kindled a fire in his eyes and gave his words an energy which pierced like daggers.

Jesus believed in the worship of God. He was careful always to maintain the forms which nourish and guard the high sentiments of the heart. His attitude to forms has often been misunderstood by persons who, glancing at the surface, have not caught the significance of what he did. He made unrelenting war upon the Pharisees who were the anointed custodians of form. He criticised their ways of fasting and giving and praying and dressing and held up their entire life to condemnation. And because of this it has been sometimes said that Jesus did not believe in forms. This is an error. Jesus did not believe in formalism. Formalism is the corpse of form — form after the spirit of life has gone out of it. Jesus hated death wherever he found it. He hated it most of all in the form of worship. Worship is the body in which reverence enshrines itself. So long as the spirit of reverence lives the worship is meaningful and beautiful; but when the spirit disappears, then the worship becomes demoralizing and corrupting. The worship of the Pharisees had lost out of it the spirit of adoration. It was cut and dried, dead, mechanical, without a heart and without a soul, and therefore odious to God and all right-thinking men. Reverence is beautiful and renders beautiful whatever form it chooses in which to express itself; but when reverence dies, then the forms of reverence become corpse-like and contaminate all who handle them. Jesus believed in forms. They are, when rightly used, the conservators of life. If you want to keep alive the spirit of courtesy and politeness, then do not cast away the forms of politeness and courtesy. If you wish to keep the fires of love burning, do not banish the forms in which love delights to express itself. If you desire to maintain the spirit of friendship, be sure you treasure all its forms. He was a wise man who advised us to keep our friendships in repair, and they who do not do this find at last that their friendships have decayed and passed away. Would you keep alive the spirit of reverence, then make use of the forms which are best adapted to feed and develop that spirit in the soul.

Jesus made fierce war on formalism, but he ever was a scrupulous observer of form. He was always in the Synagogue on the Sabbath day. He followed faithfully the order of the service. He repeated the prayers, he sang the psalms, he listened to the reading of the Scriptures. When he fed the five thousand men on the other side of Jordan he was careful to return thanks to God before the meal proceeded. When he stood at the grave of Lazarus, he first looked to God in prayer before he spoke the words, "Come forth!" In the upper chamber he observed the forms of the Passover, omitting nothing from the ritual, sacred because transmitted through so many generations. The soul of Jesus was reverent. He found it easy to bend the knee. It was natural for him to look up. He looked into his Father's face, saying at every step, "Lo, I come to do Thy will, O God!"

Here, then, we have a virtue upon whose beauty we should often fix our eyes. We do not have as much reverence as we ought to have. We are not by nature or by training a reverent people. There are those who say we become less reverent as the years go on. The older people are constantly lamenting that they miss a certain beautiful respectfulness, a lovely reverence which were more common many years ago. There are wide areas of American society from which the spirit of reverence has been banished. Men and women in many a circle are clever, interesting, brilliant, but they lack one of the three dimensions of life — they have no reach upward. Their conversation sparkles, but it is frivolous and often flippant. Their talk is witty, but the wit is often at the expense of high and sacred things. He has come far down in the scale of being who in order to display his powers finds it necessary to ridicule those things which have been prized by all good men. When one enters the world of our present-day reformers he is impressed by the large number who lack the upward look. Many of these men are tremendously in earnest, they see the crying evils of the world; their sympathies are wide and their zeal is hot, but they have no sky above their heads. They aim to glorify no Father who is in heaven. Some of them claim to admire the Man of Nazareth. They extol his character and his teachings. Yet, strange to say, they do not imitate his reverence, or cast a single glance in the direction in which his eyes were always looking. One finds this lack of reverence even in the church. In every community there are those who treat the house of God as they treat a street-car, entering it and leaving it when they please. Even habitual church attendants often surprise and shock one by their irreverent behavior in the house of prayer. Those persons are not ignoramuses or barbarians; they are simply undeveloped in the virtue of reverence.

Why is it that reverence is apparently in a state of decadence? Is it due to our improper reading? The press is constantly exploiting the sordid side of human nature, calling our attention to moral collapse and degradation, and it may be that our familiarity with vice in its varied forms is taking off the edge of our sensibility so that we no longer respond readily to the things which are noble and high. What has the stage to do — do you think — with our loss of reverence? It is lamentable that so large a proportion of plays move in that border-land which lies between decency and indecency. The openly immoral play cannot as yet be endured, but the play that is most popular is often a play which skirts the edges of the realms of the indecent. Theatre audiences seem to like a sentence now and then which looks in the direction of the unclean, and to relish an occasional insinuation or remark which leads down to the mud. Our imagination may be so coarsened by the realms through which it travels as to lose the capacity for feeling the rapture of the sense of awe.

Possibly we are becoming less reverent because we are ashamed of being afraid of anybody or anything. Fear is one of the elements in reverence, and there is a popular impression that all fear is degrading. Fear is of two kinds, — there is a godly fear and a fear which is ungodly. The latter has terror in it and throws a shadow and brings a chill.

But there is a fear which all unspoiled spirits feel in the presence of the high and holy. If mortal man, stained and marred by sin, is not awed by the thought of a Holy God, it is because he has lost the power of feeling. If there is a fear which degrades and paralyzes, there is also a fear which cleanses and exalts. The fear of the Lord is not only a virtue to be coveted by men, it is a grace lacking which angels and archangels would be incomplete. Reverence is the atmosphere of heaven. Let us come often then to the reverent Man of Nazareth who by his awe-struck obeisance to his Heavenly Father shames us out of our irreverence and makes it easier for the heart to kneel.

XXV: THE HOLINESS OF JESUS

"Which of you convicteth me of sin?"
— John viii: 46.

Here for the first time in this course of sermons I use a word which belongs to another vocabulary. Courage, humility, patience, poise, brotherliness, indignation — these all belong to a common class, but you pass the boundaries into another region when you use the word "holiness." All the other words which I have used can be applied to many of the great men of the earth; the word "holiness" can be applied to one only. Write the word "holiness" before the names of the great poets. Speak these words: "The holiness of Homer," "of Dante," "of Shakespeare," "of Tennyson." The heart revolts against it. Write the word "holiness" before the names of the great philosophers: "The holiness of Socrates," "of Plato," "of Kant," "of Herbert Spencer." There is something which offends the soul. Write the word "holiness" before the names of the great scientists: "The holiness of Newton," "of Kepler," "of Pasteur," "of Huxley," and the word does not fit those illustrious names. Speak of the holiness of the Duke of Wellington, of General Gordon, of Ulysses S. Grant, of Stonewall Jackson, and here again there is something in us which takes offence. Try the word now before the very greatest statesmen of the world: "The holiness of Pitt," "of Cavour," "of Gladstone," "of Webster," and here again we have not used the proper word. But when you say the "holiness of Jesus," that seems altogether proper. There is but one name in human history with which we can link that glorious noun.

What do we mean by holiness? We mean wholeness, full-orbed perfection. A holy man is a man without a fleck or flaw, a character without a blemish or a stain. Let us think about the sinlessness of Jesus. When we speak of the sinlessness of Jesus a thoughtful man might ask the question: "How do you know that he was sinless? You have only an account of his words and deeds, and while these may be above all criticism, how do you know what took place in the chambers of the heart? How do you know that every feeling was free from sin, that not a single thought was stained, that every motive, even the deepest, was according to the will of God? Do you not pass into the region of conjecture when you say that here was an absolutely sinless man?" And the further fact might also be urged that we have the story of only a fraction of his life. He died at the age of thirty-three, and of this period thirty years are well-nigh a total blank. Even if you grant that his public life was perfect, how can you speak with authority concerning the life which he lived before he appeared at Jordan to be baptized by John? How do you know what his life was as a boy, as a youth, as a young man? Of all this period scarcely a syllable is told us, and yet how many sins may have been committed in those seething, tempestuous years? And one might go on to say: "How can you be sure that all that he did and said recorded in the New Testament was absolutely right in the sight of God? When he denounced the Pharisees and hurled his cutting epithets at them, can you be sure there was no excess of passion? When he drove the traders from the Temple, can you be certain that he did not overstep the boundaries of righteous indignation? When he cursed the fig tree, was there no impatience in his words? When he drove the Syro-Phoenician woman away with the remark that it was not fitting to take the children's bread and cast it unto dogs, was he not guilty of the very sin which disfigured and disgraced so many of his countrymen? And then again how can you be sure that he fulfilled every duty? Even granting that we cannot charge him with any sins of commission, how do you know there were no sins of omission? Duty is infinite. There are duties toward God and toward one's fellow-men and toward one's own soul, and who in this world is competent to say that Jesus fulfilled every duty to himself and to men and to God up to the level of perfection?" These are natural questions, and questions which deserve an answer. They will occur to thoughtful minds whenever they approach the question of Jesus' holiness.

In answer to these questions it may be said in the first place that so far as we can discover there is nothing in Jesus' consciousness which indicates that he was guilty of any sin. There is no trace anywhere of regret, no indication anywhere of remorse. From first to last he is serene, jubilant, confident, free, so far as we can see, from that shadow which the consciousness of sin always casts. Now everybody agrees that Jesus was a good man, exceedingly good, extraordinarily good. Everybody admits that he was the best man that ever lived. But if we once admit this, we are bound to go a great deal farther, for just in proportion as a man is really good does he become sensitive to sin; just in proportion as his spiritual sense is keen does his consciousness of sin become disturbing and appalling. If you want the saddest confessions of shortcomings, do not go to the worst men, but to the best. The higher a man rises in spiritual attainment, the more is he cast down by the knowledge of his sins. Run through the Scriptures, and you will find that all the saints have their faces in the dust. Isaiah has a vision of God and his first cry is, "Woe is me, for I am undone!" Job has a vision of God, and he casts himself upon the ground, saying, "I abhor myself and repent in sackcloth and ashes." John the beloved disciple says, "If we say we have no sin, we deceive ourselves, and the truth is not in us." Paul the greatest of all the apostles cries out in an agony of remorse, "I am the chief of sinners." Peter says, "Depart from me, for I am a sinful man, O Lord." There is no exception in the whole list from Abraham down to the latest of the apostles. Every heart cries out in the language of the Psalmist: "Have mercy upon me, O God, and blot out my transgressions," "Wash me from mine iniquity, and cleanse me from my sin, for my sin is ever before me."

If, therefore, Jesus is indeed the best man that ever lived and still a sinner, he must have been conscious of his sin; and if he had been an honest man, conscious of his sin, he would not have concealed the fact from those that were nearest to him. He would have given signs of repentance and shown traces of regret. There would have been many an evidence of contrition and compunction. But so far as any of the apostles knew there never escaped his lips a cry for pardon. On the other hand he was always giving utterance to words like these: "He that hath seen me hath seen the Father," "I do always those things which are pleasing unto him," "Which one of you convicteth me of sin?" And even when in sight of the cross, with death only a few hours away, he looks into God's face saying, "I have finished the work which thou gavest me to do." Other men looked into the unstained splendor, the white radiance of the world eternal, and fell back abashed and condemned; Jesus looks into that same unspotted glory and says, "I have finished the work which thou gavest me to do." This is remarkable, altogether unique. Here is a man who told others to say when they prayed, "Forgive us our debts as we forgive our debtors," but he never prayed that prayer himself. Other men, even the strongest, have asked others to pray for them — he never asked prayers of any man. If then we are willing to listen to the consciousness of Jesus, we are bound to confess that here was a man without sin. If he was not without sin, then he was not a good man at all, for he carefully concealed from his companions the stained parts of his life, and led them to think that he was better than he was, in which case he was a hypocrite and our hero has vanished.

But this is not all. Not only did he hold himself immeasurably above the heads of all other men, but he forgave sins, he spoke as one having authority. No other man had ever exercised such a prerogative. Even the worst sinners when penitent at his feet received from him authoritative assurance of forgiveness. Moreover he was a man without a human ideal. All good men have looked up to some man better than themselves; Jesus looked up to no man. He placed himself above Moses. He said, "A greater than Solomon is here." He said to men, "Follow me, I am the ideal." And at the same time he said, "Be ye perfect even as your Father in heaven is perfect." How will you put these two exhortations together? "Follow me! Be ye perfect!" He was inexorable at this point, — he would not allow any one to get between him and the soul. It was worth while for a man to die for his sake — the very dearest friend a man had was to be given second place. He claimed to be first. If he were indeed perfect, all this was right; but if he were a sinner concealing his sin or unconscious of his sin, then all such exhortations as, "Follow me," are demoralizing, and his pretensions are blasphemous. If he was good at all, he was sinless. Attention ought to be called to the impression which he made upon others. The men who were nearest to him got the idea that he was without sin. When he came to John the Baptist asking to be baptized, John drew back from him, saying: "I cannot baptize you. You ought to baptize me." And why? Because John was baptizing men for their sins. He could not baptize Jesus, because Jesus had no sins. And when Jesus makes his reply, he does not say, "I am a sinner, therefore I must be baptized," he says, "Suffer it now, for it is becoming that we should fulfil all righteousness." There was a reason why the baptism should be performed, — there was another element in baptism besides confession of sin. John was the beloved disciple, coming the nearest to the Master's heart. In the third chapter of his first letter he says this, "He was manifested to take away our sin, and in him is no sin." That was the impression which the Lord made upon him. Peter was one of his most loyal friends. He was with him day and night through three years. In the second chapter of his first letter he says, "He did no sin, neither was guile found in his mouth." Now these men were with Jesus. They ate with him, drank with him, slept with him, they saw him in all conditions and in all moods, and under varying circumstances. They saw him hungry, angry, stern, surprised, disappointed, amazed, yet they believed that in him there was no sin. The writer to the Hebrews in the fourth chapter reminds his readers that while Jesus was tempted in all points as we are, yet he was without sin. That was the impression then which was made upon the church. After the resurrection — they worshipped him as God. It is inconceivable that in so short a time a great body of intelligent men and women should have been worshipping him as God and singing hymns of praise to him if he had not made upon them the impression that he was holy.

Here, then, we have reached the crowning characteristic of Jesus. It is this which differentiates him from all other men who have ever lived. Every other man has known the pang of remorse, every other man has cried for pardon. Simon Peter was hounded by memories; he was a good man, a great man, a tireless worker in the church, but condemning memories pursued him down through the years, and when at last the time came to die he said, "Crucify me with my head downward." He said this because he remembered his sin. Paul was a good man and a great man, but he was hounded by condemning memories. He filled the days and nights with work for God, but he could never forget that he had been a persecutor of the church, and so he entered heaven feeling that he was the chief of sinners. Never has there been but one white soul, never but one life unspotted, never but one mind without a stain, never but one heart perfect. It is this sinlessness which gives Jesus his power. You cannot understand the New Testament unless you acknowledge that he was holy. His life was one of suffering, persecution, ending in a horrible death, but yet the New Testament is a joyous book. There is no gloom in it because there was no gloom in him. His soul was radiant. Nothing creates gloom in this world but sin. All the things which we count terrible are insignificant and have no power to cast a shadow. There is only one thing which makes the spirit droop, and that is sin. His sinlessness explains his joyfulness. He said, "No man knows the Father but the son" — and why. Because "Blessed are the pure in heart, for they shall see God." Because his heart was stainless, his vision of the Eternal was unclouded. He knew God as no other man has ever known him. And it was this sinlessness which was the secret of his fascination. He drew men to him, they hung upon his words, they were fascinated by him even when they hated, they were drawn to him even when they feared him. Simon Peter expresses the conflicting emotions of the heart in, "Depart from me, for I am a sinful man, O Lord." When Jesus asks him whether he is going away he says, "To whom shall we go; thou hast the words of eternal life." The reason we are drawn to him is not because of his courage, his sympathy, his patience, or his brotherliness; it is because we feel instinctively that he is far above us, a man without a sin. It is this which gives the Christian church its power. The Christian church has but one perfect possession, that is Jesus. The creed of the church is not perfect, its phrases were formed by the blundering mind of man. The Bible is not perfect, it is not inerrant, it has many a flaw. The church itself is imperfect, stained through and through with sin; but Jesus of Nazareth, the head of the church, is stainless. And because he is without sin the church will come off triumphant.

If you ask why it is that men are separated from Jesus, it is because he is sinless and they are not. Some of you are not interested in him; it is because he is so far above you. Some of you have no sympathy with him; it is because you are not at all like him. Some of you do not understand his words; that is because you are disobedient. Some of you have no disposition to do his will; it is because you are the prisoners of sin. But the sinless Christ does not turn away from us, no matter how sinful we are. He says: "Come unto me. He that cometh unto me I will in no wise cast out." Without sin himself he can pity us in our sin, and is willing to wash away the stains. He is the Lamb of God that taketh away the sin of the world.

But Thee, but Thee, O sovereign Seer of time,
But Thee, O poet's Poet, Wisdom's Tongue,
But Thee, O man's best Man, O love's best Love,
O perfect life in perfect labor writ,
O all men's Comrade, Servant, King, or Priest, —
What if or yet, what mole, what flaw, what lapse,
What least defect or shadow of defect,
What rumor, tattled by an enemy,
Of inference loose, what lack of grace
Even in torture's grasp, or sleep's, or death's —
Oh, what amiss may I forgive in Thee,
Jesus, good Paragon, thou Crystal Christ?

XXVI: THE GREATNESS OF JESUS

"His name shall be called Wonderful."
— Isaiah ix: 6.

What is greatness? Who is a great man? What is the distinctive element in a man which gives him this proud distinction? The dictionaries will not help us. We find it difficult to draw a verbal line between the great man and the man who is not great. And yet the muse of history has no difficulty in picking out individuals here and there on whose heads she places crowns. With a bold hand she inscribes certain names upon the shining list, and bids coming generations revere these names as those of the world's immortals. If it is difficult to write a definition of greatness, there seems to be no difficulty in finding men whom the heart persists in counting great.

When we scrutinize the faces of this immortal company, we are struck by the variety of gifts and graces. No two of these men are alike. Homer is not like Phidias, nor is Phidias like Pericles, nor is Pericles like Plato. Virgil is different from Caesar, who is different from Dante, and Dante is not at all like Scipio or Raphael or Justinian. Goethe is different from Frederick the Great, and the latter is different from Kant and Hegel, and these two are not like either Mendelssohn or Bismarck. Napoleon and La Place and Racine and Pasteur are all different types of men. William the Conqueror is not like Shakespeare, nor is Bishop Butler like Newton, nor is the Duke of Wellington like Gladstone. Franklin is different from Washington, and Lincoln is different from Longfellow, and Fulton and Morse are different from all. And yet all these are enrolled among the mighty dead. In what respect were they alike? What characteristic is common to all? In such a heterogeneous company is it possible to find any mark which makes them akin? It is possible, and the quality which is common to all is an extraordinary capacity for achievement. These men all did things, enduring things, so that the world was not the same after they had gotten done with it. They carved statues or painted pictures or led armies or ruled states or composed music or framed laws or wrote poems or made discoveries or inventions which enriched the lives and homes of men. They achieved something worth while. They made a mark on the mind of the world. The product of their genius is an imperishable possession of our race.

Was Jesus great? What did he achieve? What did he ever do? He never chiselled a statue or painted a picture or wrote a poem or composed a piece of music or constructed a philosophical system or published a book or led an army or controlled a senate or framed a law or made a discovery or contrived an invention or did any one of the things which have made the names of other men illustrious. He never wore a crown or held a sceptre or threw round his shoulders a purple robe. He never held an office either in church or state. He did absolutely nothing in art, literature, science, philosophy, invention, statesmanship or war, the seven kingdoms in which the world's great men have won their crowns. And yet everybody calls Jesus great. No informed man in any part of the world would to-day deny him that exalting adjective. Not only is he counted great, but in a large part of the world he is counted greatest — so great that no one else can be compared with him. Charles Lamb gave expression to the feeling of us all when he said, "If Shakespeare was to come into this room, we should all rise up to meet him; but if Christ was to come into it, we should all fall upon our knees." His greatness is greater than that of all others, and it is also different.

Other men are great artists or poets or generals or statesmen, whereas Jesus is a great man. His greatness lies in the realm of personality, in the kingdom of character. His achievement was not wrought with paint or with chisel or with sword or with pen, but by the heavenly magic of a victorious will. There is nothing of him but his manhood. He wore none of the spangled robes of earth. We do not say, "Behold the poet, the orator, the philosopher, the general, the statesman, the sovereign, we say, Behold the Man!" A man may be a great general and still not be a great man. Alexander the Great got his title from his genius for massing phalanxes of soldiers and hurling them with irresistible fury against the army which opposed him. As a man he was a weakling. Passion wrecked him before noon. Napoleon the Great was great as a leader of armies, but as a man he was petty and vain and despicable. As a murderer and robber he was great, but as a man he was a pygmy. Great statesmen have not always been great men. Sometimes they have been unscrupulous and cowardly, their whole interior life degraded by appetites and passions which have made them underlings and slaves. The great artists of the world have not all been kings and queens in the graces of manhood and womanhood. It is one of the saddest of all surprises to discover on reading the biographies of the world's immortal workers how many of them have been narrow and superstitious, selfish and envious, sordid in their ambitions and groveling in their aims, achieving one significant or beautiful piece of work in the glory of which the shabbiness of their character has been swallowed up. Jesus was great in his soul. The dimensions of his mind and his heart were colossal. His spirit was regal, august, sublime.

How he looms above the heads of his contemporaries! There were men of distinction in Palestine nineteen centuries ago. Jesus measured his strength with the greatest men of his land and generation. But how lacking these men were in insight the Gospels everywhere disclose. They fumbled cardinal questions and stumbled at points which were critical. They lost themselves in the mazes of problems which they could not see through or master. Jesus had eyes which saw to the core of every problem and to the centre of every situation. He never missed the essential point or was misled by a subordinate issue. He stripped off the accidental from the soul of the essential, and no matter how tangled or complicated a matter was he seized the dominant principle and made all things plain. Compared with him the Scribes and Pharisees were owls batting their stupid eyes in the glare of noon. Insight is a trait of greatness. Only great men see deep into things. It was his insight which made him formidable to the men who tried to trip and trap him with their questions. Again and again they tried it, but they never succeeded. He always outwitted their subtlety, and always discomfited them at their favorite game. Whenever they dashed at him with a question intended to roll him in the dust, he seized it, turned its point upon the man who asked it, and went on his way triumphant. Never did they get the advantage of him in a discussion or an argument. No more clever man ever lived. He beat his assailants into silence every time they attacked him. His cleverness was too much for the acutest intellect which wrestled with him. He was quick, dexterous, adroit, and yet when we think of him we do not think of his cleverness because cleverness is a scintillation of the intellect, and while intellectual brilliancy dazzles us in other men, we are not impressed by it in Jesus because his cleverness is only one of many talents and endowments which combine to add lustre to his princely, transcendent personality. In ambition and ideal he was in comparison with the leaders of his people what Mont Blanc is to the chalets which farmers have erected at its base.

His greatness comes out in his fellowship with his disciples. They were strong and able men, all of them, able later on to turn the world upside down; but they cut a sorry figure in the presence of the man they acknowledge to be their master. They are pitifully and incorrigibly stupid. They cannot understand some of the simplest things the Master says. He is so high above them that they cannot climb to where he is. There is pathos in his oft-repeated question, "Do you not yet understand?" But it is in their temper and ambition that the disciples are at their worst. They were petty, envious, selfish men. They wrangled among themselves as to which one of them should hold the highest place, and even on the last evening of Jesus' life they squabbled as to the places they should occupy around the table. No wonder he calls them "little children," for that was all they were. They were childish in their temper and ambitions just as most men are. They Were as old in years as Jesus; but in thought and aim, in hope and ideal, they were as compared with Jesus only a company of babies.

When we leave the New Testament and walk among the nations of the earth where shall we find a man with whom we should be willing to compare Jesus of Nazareth? Can you think of an Italian or a German or a Frenchman or an Englishman or an American whose name is worthy to be linked with his? The heart draws back shuddering at the suggestion of such a thought. Great men have come and gone, doing their mighty deeds and leaving behind names which shall not die, but what race or nation would dare even in its most egotistic and vainglorious moments to suggest that the most illustrious of all its sons has a right to sit on a throne so high as the throne of Jesus? His soul is like a star and dwells apart. He is unique, unapproached, unapproachable. He is the incomparable. His name is Wonderful.

How great Jesus is can be told by the length and width and depth of his achievement. Greatness is measured by the effect which it produces. Men cannot be judged by stature or physical characteristics. You cannot tell whether a man is great or not by looking at his body. All men are in body substantially alike. They have the same appetites, passions, organs. If you tickle them they laugh, if you prick them they bleed. Nor can you find a man's greatness always in his words. For all men use substantially the same nouns and adjectives, verbs and adverbs. The same sentence spoken by two men may have totally different results. One man speaks it, and it produces no impression. It dies in the moment of its birth. Another speaks it and it sets hearts blazing and is remembered for evermore. Greatness does not lie in words but in souls. Not even do a man's actions reveal completely what he is. In their conduct great men act much as do ordinary men. It is for this reason that no man is ever a hero to his valet. The valet hears his master's words, sees the clothes he wears, the things he eats, the engagements which he keeps, and knowing these he cannot believe that his master is a hero. A valet's eyes do not see to the ends of things, nor can a valet's mind weigh effects or trace the track of influence. He does not know what his master is accomplishing in the world, but it is by the total effect of a man's life that we are to tell whether or not he is great. Great men are all alike in this, that they bring things to pass. Things take place when they are present which do not take place in their absence. They change the currents of men's thoughts and set a new fashion in the world. Men gather round them and criticise them, point out where they fall short, and show how the thing could have been better done in some other way; but the critics die and are forgotten and the great man lives on forever. How he accomplishes his results he never tells. Why he exerts such an influence, we never know. The secret of greatness is incommunicable. It lies hidden in the abysmal deeps of personality.

If Jesus is to be judged by the effects which he produced and still produces, then his name is indeed Wonderful. Upon the men of his time he exerted a power so marvellous that it seemed uncanny, magical, and some people thought he must be in league with the mighty powers of the under world. When he spoke men overflowed with ideas and feelings — feelings of love or feelings of detestation. No man ever stood stolid in his presence. Men went wild over him, some in adoration and some in hatred. Wherever he went he left men seething and bubbling. There were a few men — his apostles — who came close to him. Upon these he exerted an influence which extended to the roots of their being. One of these men — Thomas — was unusually slow and cool. He was not made of inflammable stuff. He was not easily carried away by emotion, for the tides of emotion in him were not strong. But this man when Jesus one day suggested going to a certain place beset with danger exclaimed, "Let us go and die with him." It is not easy to die at thirty. No normal man in his ordinary mood wants to die before the sun has reached the meridian. But this man Thomas had been so wrought upon by the personality of Jesus that he was ready to die with him. And so were all the apostles. Peter in the upper chamber declared with emphasis that he was ready to go with Jesus to prison and to death. A few hours later his courage oozed out, but that cowardice was only temporary, and Peter later on did the very thing which he declared to Jesus he would do. And what Peter did all of the apostles did, John alone excepted. He has indeed something extraordinary within him who can so work upon the minds and hearts of men as to make them glad to give up their lives for him. There is only one greater thing than dying for another and that is living for another, living a life of obloquy and persecution, suffering all things for his sake. Here is the climax of power. Jesus changed men. He changed their habits and opinions and ambitions, he changed their tempers and dispositions and natures. He changed their hearts. They were never the same after they gave themselves up to him. God and man, the world and duty, were different to them after they had looked steadily into his face. Wherever he went he transformed human lives. He transfigured human faces by cleansing the fountains of the heart. This is greatness indeed.

And what he did in Palestine he has been doing ever since. Wherever the story of his life is carried the climate of thought and feeling changes. Every land across which his name has been heralded has been transformed in ideals and institutions. The forward-looking portion of the world numbers the years from the date of his birth. Richter was not writing poetry but prose when he declared that Jesus' pierced hands lifted empires off their hinges and turned the stream of history into a new channel. You cannot account for the difference between Occident and Orient without a consideration of the influence of this one Man. Fifteen hundred years ago the civilization of China was what it is to-day. The social and industrial orders have through all this period remained there unchanged, and Chinese society is no more highly embellished and the Chinese character is not a whit more cultivated than they were a millennium and a half ago. Fifteen hundred years ago northern Europe was a wilderness, and so also was the island of Britain. In these wildernesses there lived various tribes of barbarous people, whose pastime was to make war on one another. Many of them were but little above the rank of savages. Through fifteen hundred years northern Europe and the British Isles have been coming up, up, up, until to-day there are no higher summits in the world. While China has remained exactly where she was, western Europe has been ascending; and when you endeavor to interpret this wonderful phenomenon, you cannot lose sight of the fact that China has been gazing into the face of Confucius while western Europe has been gazing into the face of Jesus. Jesus of

Nazareth has lifted Europe to the seats of power. It is one of the supreme miracles of the world's history.

Some men are great in their influence for a generation, and then their power begins to wane. They sit on thrones for a season and then abdicate. Will it be so with Jesus? We only know that through nineteen hundred years he has been climbing to a supremacy increasingly spacious and august. His name has been rising, swallowing up the glory of other names as the sun mounting the eastern sky swallows up the stars. To-day his name is above every name. Ours is the greatest of all the centuries. Never have men been so impatient to get on as they are to-day, and never have they been so indifferent to the past. And yet the most thrilling cry of our day is, "Back to Jesus!" It is heard all around the world. Men once cried, "Back to the Reformers!" but the Reformers did not satisfy, and then the cry was, "Back to the Fathers!" but the Fathers could not help, and then the cry was, "Back to the Apostles!" but the Apostles were found to be shining only with a reflected light, and so now the world is saying: "Back to Jesus!" "Let us go back to him for the sake of getting on, in order to get light for our darkened pathway, and to find principles with which to solve our complicated problems!" More lives of Jesus have been written within the last fifty years than of any other historic character. More pages are printed about him every week than about any hundred of the world's greatest men. He exerts a power which is so phenomenal that many feel he must be more than man, linked in some way or other with the Eternal. He must be — men say — the Son of God. In this land alone men contribute two hundred million dollars every year to support the institutions which bear his name. They are not compelled to do this. They do it voluntarily because they want to do it, and because he so works upon them that they count such giving a privilege and pleasure. As Napoleon Bonaparte once said, "This man vanished for eighteen hundred years still holds the characters of men as in a vice." The little Corsican sat dumfounded as he compared his greatness with the greatness of the Man of Galilee. Napoleon's last biographer devotes two volumes to the rise of his hero and two volumes to his decline and fall. All the volumes of the life of Jesus record the story of his ascent. He goes on and on from victory to victory, from glory to glory, and as men's eyes become cleansed and their hearts purified they see with increasing certainty that God has indeed so highly exalted him that some day every knee shall bend to him and every tongue confess that he is King indeed.

His greatness is full-orbed. He was complete, and in his completeness we find an explanation of his beauty. Men who stood nearest to him were charmed and swayed by his loveliness. He was full of grace and truth. He had a charm about him which wooed and fascinated. Children liked him, boys sang for him, publicans hung upon him. He had the heart of a child, the tenderness of a woman, the strength of a man. The three dimensions of his life were complete. He had eyes which looked along extended lines running into eternity; he had sympathies wide enough to cover humanity to its outermost edge; he had a purpose which included all lands and ages, his kingdom is to be universal and it shall have no end. He is at every point complete. His virtues are all full-statured, his graces are all in fullest bloom. You can no more add anything to him than you can add something to the sky. He pushed every good trait of human character to its utmost limit. His forgiveness was unbounded, his generosity was untiring, his patience was inexhaustible, his mercy was immeasurable, his courage was illimitable, his wisdom was unfathomable, his kindness was interminable, his faith removed mountains, his hope had no shadow in it, his love was infinite. And so it is impossible to go beyond him. We can never outgrow him. He will be always ahead of us. We shall always hear him saying, "Follow me!" He is the ideal of the heart. He is the goal of humanity. It is this completeness of his character which accounts not only for his beauty but for his perennial and increasing power. He is the lily of the valley, the fairest of ten thousand, the one altogether lovely. He is the image of God!

"If Jesus Christ is a man,
And only a man, I say,
That of all mankind I cleave to him,
And to him will I cleave alway.

"If Jesus Christ is a God,
And the only God, I swear,
I will follow him through heaven and hell,
The earth, the sea, and the air."

A NOTE TO THE READER

WE HOPED YOU LOVED THIS BOOK. IF YOU DID, PLEASE LEAVE A REVIEW ON AMAZON TO LET EVERYONE ELSE KNOW WHAT YOU THOUGHT.

WE WOULD ALSO LIKE TO THANK OUR SPONSORS **WWW.DIGITALHISTORYBOOKS.COM** WHO MADE THE PUBLICATION OF THIS BOOK POSSIBLE.

WWW.DIGITALHISTORYBOOKS.COM PROVIDES A WEEKLY NEWSLETTER OF THE BEST DEALS IN HISTORY AND HISTORICAL FICTION.

SIGN UP TO THEIR NEWLSETTER TO FIND OUT MORE ABOUT THEIR LATEST DEALS.

Made in the USA
Las Vegas, NV
19 November 2023